The Alchemy of

PURPOSE

Learn to Love and Live with Purpose

by Mark Mittlesteadt

THE ALCHEMY OF PURPOSE

Learn to Love and Live with Purpose

The Artist Within
www.the-artist-within.com
markm@the-artist-within.com

ISBN: 978-1-7345335-0-7

Cover Design by Dawn and Mark Mittlesteadt

Printed in the United States of America.

This book is dedicated to all those who struggle to find meaning and purpose in life. Know that above all else, you are loved. When we learn to fully love ourselves, just as we are, the Universe opens the world of possibilities, and through our imagination, we express this love, manifesting our greatest purpose.

TABLE OF CONTENTS

ACKNOWLEDGMENTS

I would like to thank my wife, Dawn Mittlesteadt, for supporting me and putting up with my crazy ideas for all these years while I found myself. She was always behind me through both the ups and downs and I would not be where I am without her. She was an angel sent to me. She offered to help me edit this book, and she made it so much better than I ever would have done had I written it alone. I would also like to thank my children, Sam, Alex, Lauren and Michelle, who taught me what is important in life. I need to single out my daughter Michelle, whose birth totally changed my life by showing me what unconditional love really is. And I want to thank my son Alex, whose life inspired me to go back to college.

I also need to thank others who inspired me along my journey, including all those who stayed with me despite my failings as a friend. Thank you, Dan Pick, a lifelong friend; Tim Winkelman, who always followed his own path; Keri Gille, a gentle soul who always remained true to himself; Dennis Kohnhorst, with whom I formed my first band, against all odds and ignoring those who thought we couldn't do it; Mike Kleinschmidt, an amazing songwriter with a deep soul who gave me the opportunity to express my own music through his own; Bill Cortright, who completely changed his life and has been a constant source of inspiration for me; and Paul Scuderi, who always followed his own path and included me in his many projects where I could explore my creative side as an artist and writer.

I want to thank my college instructors who, when I went back to school late in life to study psychology, were extremely helpful with their feedback, constant encouragement and thought-provoking dialogue. They were professional therapists as well as professors, and as such they helped me uncover issues in my life and figure out not only who I am and why I am the way I am, but provided me with a deeper understanding of human behavior in general.

Of course, I want to thank the family I grew up with. To my father, Norman, who was practical and taught me the skills to invent, build and repair, and to appreciate the outdoors. To my mother, Faye, a working artist and a wonderful human being who inspired me more than anyone in my life. I miss you both, and I am grateful and fortunate to have you as parents. To my brothers, Bruce and Breck, for being there as I was growing up, and to my dear, sweet sister Chris, whose selflessness, caring and devotion to family is unmatched. No matter how far apart we lived, you were always there for me. I love you all.

I owe a special debt of gratitude to Estella Arias, who inspired me to see purpose in a new light, which helped make this book all that it is.

Two wonderful people need to be acknowledged for helping make this book all it could be, and they are Shanda Trofe at Transcendent Publishing for her guidance, and my fabulous editor Dana Micheli for her tremendous talent, skill and dedication to it.

I also want to thank everyone who came into my life, directly or indirectly, for good or for bad, for giving me clarity and understanding. This includes every creative human being who came before me, who influenced and inspired me with their devotion to their respective crafts. I thank everyone who has ever sought my counsel. You helped me even as I helped you, and my study of human behavior would not be complete without you. I apologize if anyone feels left out, but the truth is it would take an entire book to thank everyone who made an impact on my life. They know who they are, and they have my undying gratitude.

Finally, I thank each of you who bought this book. I hope you find some inspiration in it.

INTRODUCTION

What if I told you our only purpose in life was Love? To love ourselves and love one another? That that's all there is to it and nothing more? Would you believe it?

Would you believe me if I told you that our purpose is to be happy? What if it were joy, contentment, peace, meaning, or fulfillment? If I told you the key to a happy life is "doing what we love," would you then believe that is our purpose?

So many are struggling to find what it is they want to do with their life that will give it meaning. How would you feel if you found out that the very thing you've been seeking your entire life doesn't exist, at least not as you've come to know it?

What is this nebulous thing called "purpose"? On paper, it looked like I had found it. I'd been doing what I love and following my dreams my entire adult life and yet, like so many others who have done the same, I hadn't found much more joy, contentment or meaning than if I hadn't pursued them. How can this be? Isn't discovering our purpose and then doing it supposed to be the recipe for a happy life?

Clearly something about our idea of purpose is erroneous or incomplete. Perhaps it is wrong entirely. After years of studying psychology and human behavior, and contemplating the meaning of purpose, I had an awakening, an epiphany that revealed something about purpose I had overlooked. This revelation would become the seed for what I call the Theory of Purpose.

By reading this book, you will come to understand that purpose isn't a thing that we do or something we seek. It is a process of living that gives meaning to our life and from which all the wonderful things we typically associate with life purpose are derived.

Most of all, our purpose is only fully realized when it is done out of Love, for ourselves and the world around us. There can be no other way to live it. Yes, cliché though it may be, Love truly is the answer.

Chapter One

WHAT IS PURPOSE?

*P*urpose has many different meanings, depending on the context. The dictionary meaning is: *The reason for which something is done or created, or for which something exists.* Or: *To have as one's intention or objective.*

Taken literally, then, purpose can be almost anything we do. Making breakfast can be our purpose because we need to feed ourselves. Purpose can also be doing what we love to do with our life because we are creating something. For obvious reasons, we each have different ideas as to what purpose means to us. That said, you may find the dictionary definition quite appropriate, specifically, *the reason for which something exists.* That something is us. Why do we exist? What is the meaning of our existence? It is in this context that we wish to discover our purpose, because we want to give our life meaning.

It would be more accurate, however, to expand our definition of purpose to encompass both meanings. Thus, our purpose is having *our intention be the reason for our existence.* But how does this definition give our life meaning?

As we can see, the entire idea of purpose is thought by most as the "what" we do with our life (as in "doing *what* we love"). This is why we're so preoccupied with finding our purpose in our work, as if this will somehow solve life's problems and we will then be forever happy. Yet, even when we do what we love, happiness is no more guaranteed than when we are doing something(s) we do not love. Clearly, *what* we do is insufficient.

We can take purpose as the "intention" in what we do, or our *objective.* Then our definition goes beyond the *what* we do, and into the *why* we do it. Yet this is still insufficient as to the true nature of purpose, because although we can explain purpose as both a thing and an objective, we are lacking a fundamental part of purpose in our existence: our actions, or *how* we live.

Taking this one step further than the dictionary meaning would explain the *how* of *what* we do, along with the *why* (our intention) in doing it. This tells us that purpose is neither just a *thing* nor an *intention*, but also an *action* playing out in our life. This gives rise to the Three Elements of Purpose: *Manifestation - What we do; Expression - How we do it; and Intention - Why we do it.* Therefore, purpose is not solely a thing, an objective, or an action, but the *process of how we experience life.*

Ask yourself these questions: What do you hope to achieve by discovering your purpose? How do you imagine your life as you live out this purpose? Will you then be happy or at peace? Will you feel content and derive meaning? What exactly allows us to discover meaning for our life, so that we experience happiness, peace, contentment, et cetera? The Theory of Purpose explains in detail what purpose really is and how our actions give our life meaning.

The Theory of Purpose

Purpose is not a singularity, but the fluid, ongoing experiential process of life. We are the manifestation of the Consciousness of the Universe, co-creating and manifesting our life into existence. What we think, we create. What we believe, we attract. What we imagine, we become. Thought, belief and imagination set our intention. In our intention, we express our purpose, manifesting our experience. Our experience creates conflict and through its resolution we achieve growth, which provides contextual meaning for our life. Our shared, universal purpose is Love, uniquely and individually expressed as a manifestation of the Consciousness of the Universe.

Chapter Two

THE ELEMENTS OF THE
THEORY OF PURPOSE

he preceding illustration depicts the Theory of Purpose through its elements. There are the Three Elements of the Mind, the Three Elements of Purpose, the Two Elements of Meaning, the Six Elements of Life, and the Four Levels of Purpose. The last and most important element is Love.

Let's explore the elements of the Theory of Purpose.

The Three Elements of the Mind

Thought   Beliefs   Imagination

Thought - The ever-expanding ideation of our life. What we think, we create.

Beliefs - The truths we hold about ourselves and the world. What we believe, we attract.

Imagination - The infinite possibilities that what we imagine, we become.

The Three Elements of Purpose

Intention   Expression   Manifestation

Intention - The singular focus of the Three Elements of the Mind.

Expression - How we uniquely and mindfully live the intention of our purpose.

Manifestation - The energy we vibrate in, thus what we create for ourselves and the world.

The Two Elements of Meaning

Conflict

Resolution

Conflict - The lessons we are given from which to learn.

Resolution - The growth from where we derive meaning.

The Six Elements of Life

Career

Finance

Health

Relationships

Spirituality

Personal Growth

Career - The tasks and occupations of our purpose.
Finance - The wealth we acquire to use for our purpose.
Health - The health we achieve through self-love.
Relationships - The infinite Love we share out of Oneness.
Spirituality - The connection to our eternal divine self.
Personal Growth - The expansion of our self in all areas of life.

The Four Levels of Purpose

Material   Ego   Altruistic   Enlightened

Material - Happiness in material possessions.
Ego - Happiness in doing what we love.
Altruistic – Joy of being in service to others.
Enlightened – Peace in seeking God.

Chapter Three

THE THREE ELEMENTS
OF THE MIND

hat we think, we create. What we believe, we attract. What we imagine, we become. Our thoughts, beliefs and imagination are the corner-stones of purpose. These Three Elements of the Mind are the foundation of everything we do in life. They control how we manifest and express our purpose. If we do not understand these elements and how to control their use, nothing in our life can change and we will not live with purpose.

Life exists entirely within our mind.

Thought

Imagine what our lives would be like if we believed in the power of thought. Imagine how much control we would have over our own life, like a wizard making all our desires come true. All our problems would disappear, and we'd be happy. Just imagine the things we could do and accomplish.

Imagine if thought was energy and we could manipulate it like an alchemist, changing and creating the world around us. Sounds wonderful, right? The truth is, we don't have to imagine it, for while our bodies and all the other physical elements in the world around us provide the evidence of our experiences, life itself exists *entirely within our mind.* Thought is indeed energy and we do change and create our life, though most of us are completely unaware we're doing so. I'll say it again: *life is nothing more than manipulated energy, transformed into the physical evidence we experience.*

Everything that exists is either energy or mass. When energy condenses into matter it becomes an object with mass, yet it still retains the energy that created it. This makes it vibrate with life. All matter, including us, resonates with this energy.

Thought is not an object with mass; therefore, it must be energy. It is this energy with which we have created our life; indeed, everything in our reality exists because of it. We use the energy of thought to manipulate the energy of the physical elements of nature, creating a world of our own making. What kind of life, what kind of physical "evidence," have you created using this energy of thought?

As mentioned above, the very first element of the Theory of Purpose is thought because *what we think, we create.* Thus, in order to understand our creations we must first understand the nature of thought itself. We were born with thought even before we had words to express it. What language did we think in before we learned the language of our family? The language of pure *energy.* What does that say about thought itself? We have the *energy of thought* upon our own creation, yet we often misuse it because we realize so little of the power it holds.

Just as our parents taught us their language so we could communicate, they taught us *how to think* and *the way we think.* Everything we think about ourselves and the world around us was programmed into us by our family until around the age of seven. Though we were born with this energy of thought, it was shaped (manipulated) in a very particular way and we carry this programmed way of thinking with us the rest of our life. Because we were never taught that our thought is energy itself, we think, and therefore live, mostly on autopilot. We live based on the erroneous belief that life is the physical evidence (i.e. what we see, touch, smell, hear and taste), rather than the energy with which it vibrates.

As a result, we are very careless with our thought. We treat it like we do our breathing – it's just there, operating in the background as we go about our daily routine. While we all *desire* more meaning in our life, we don't all *actively seek* it. For every thought we have, there is a deeper meaning behind it, to which we pay little attention. We are forever onto the next thought; thus, we're never really living in the present moment. Couple that with our belief that life exists outside of us, in the physical world, and it's no wonder that our thoughts are born largely out of reaction instead of intention.

In order to create the life we desire, we must be aware of our thought. This awareness is called mindfulness. Mindfulness is *paying attention to our intention*. When we are mindful of the energy behind our thought, we are able to manipulate this energy in any manner we choose. We have the ability to intentionally use the energy of thought to create anything we wish. However, when we live according to our programming, we are reacting to what we observe in the physical world and thus recreating it whether we desire to or not. We'll have a thought to do something and then we go about performing the task without any mindfulness about it. We are then as reactionary in our actions as we are in our thought and we will have very little control over how our life turns out. We will just keep repeating the same routine over and over again and tell ourselves this is "just the way life is." We may even look at others who have the lives we think we want and tell ourselves that they are the lucky few, that they hit the jackpot in this "random" universe. We don't realize that when we think this way, we are creating more of the same. Remember, what we think, we create. Knowing this is power.

*Belief is the collection of thoughts that becomes
our truth, even when it is not true.*

Beliefs

Imagine if we truly believed we could manipulate everything with the energy of thought. Imagine if we believed that the physical evidence we have been programmed to rely on can be changed and transformed by virtue of our thoughts. Imagine we could see what we have created thus far as mere reflections of the erroneous beliefs we have held.

Belief is not always truth. It simply becomes *our own truth* through repetitive thought. Belief *does not require evidence* to support it. If it did, we would not believe in God. There is no evidence that God exists, yet it is a truth billions around the world hold to be true. We can believe in God, and that we are a creation of God, yet we refuse to believe in our limitless potential. I am reminded of an observation made by comedian George Carlin: *"Tell people there's an invisible man in the sky who created the universe, and the vast majority will believe you. Tell them the paint is wet, and they have to touch it."* This is human nature. Most will only "believe it when they can see it," when we should hold as our truth, "We will see it when we believe it." We attract everything from our beliefs, even when there is no evidence to justify it as truth.

If we are ill, we can believe ourselves to be ill because the evidence supports it. It is our truth *and* it is in fact true. However, if we are ill but hold the belief that we will be well, using the energy behind our thought, we will attract wellness; we can manipulate the physical elements to create the health we desire. Remember, life exists entirely within our mind, and what we see and experience in the physical world is merely a reflection of that inner life.

This is how it is with all our beliefs. If we believe we are incapable of accomplishing something, we will remain incapable, whether this is true or not. If we believe we are ugly, this is our truth and we will not recognize our beauty. If we believe we are failures, we will continue to fail. If we believe in our limitations, whether they are real or not, we will be limited. These faulty beliefs are simply a collection of thoughts we hold in our mind and because thought is energy, we manipulate this energy into the evidence we experience.

However, we can change our beliefs and attract more of what we really want. That means that even if you've always held the belief that, "I am ugly," you can decide to use the energy behind your thought to change that belief to "I am beautiful." With time and practice, your new perception will change in your mind and you will then see yourself as beautiful. If your current truth tells you that you are a failure, you can choose to stop believing that and instead believe you are successful, and you will then attract success. Your *current reality* is merely evidence of your *current truth*, or belief. If you want to change your current reality, you must believe in an alternate future reality that you will at some point attract. If you continue to cling to your current beliefs, consciously or subconsciously, your current reality will continue to dictate your future. The power to manipulate energy into the form you desire truly does lie within you, just like an alchemist manipulates the energy within the elements of nature.

Some people never grow beyond their beliefs, and so they will never see themselves as the beautiful beings they are; they will never see the world as a beautiful manifestation of their mind. Their beliefs are not rooted in truth, but they have become *their truth*. This is the power of thought and beliefs. Contemplate every belief you hold — about yourself, the world around you, and God (or higher being, or whatever words you wish to use).

Are these beliefs really true, or are they simply thoughts you've been programmed to buy into? How can you be sure?

Consider that the more energy you put into faulty thinking, the more you will hold onto faulty beliefs. Because thought is energy, our beliefs are very much tied to our feelings; in fact, even when our beliefs are harmful, we often hold onto them with strong emotional energy. That said, beliefs can also hold a tremendous amount of positive energy that are healthy and empowering for us.

Beliefs hold the energy of thought. Remember, The Theory of Purpose states that *"what we think we create and what we believe we attract."* What we attract can be positive or negative, because our beliefs will always attract the same energy they hold.

The law of attraction states that "like attracts like." This means that our physical experience directly correlates to the level at which we are thinking, believing or — energetically speaking — vibrating. It stands to reason, then, that what we attract is not always what we want, but it is always what we *need.* Sometimes what we need are lessons that provide us with opportunities to change our beliefs and, therefore, our reality. Of course, depending on our present circumstances, these lessons can feel less like an opportunity and more like a hardship, but if we look below the surface we'll inevitably find a kernel of knowledge we were meant to uncover so that we may do things differently moving forward.

One way we can change our programmed thoughts and beliefs is by using the third element of our mind: our imagination.

Imagination is the playground of the mind, where fantasy is our reality and life is the illusion.

Imagination

We were born with the ability to think but free of preconceived beliefs, and so as children we had no need to discern reality from what we held in our imagination. To us, our imagination was just as real as anything else. Didn't we as children fear the monsters under our bed, even though there was no evidence they existed? We did not require the monsters to materialize to affirm our belief in them. Perhaps the fears were unfounded or represented other issues, but they were our reality in that moment nonetheless. Santa Clause, the Easter Bunny, and other storybook characters that came to life in our mind's eye were as real as they were imagined. In these early years of life we continued to play with our imagination even as we became programmed, and sometimes in spite of it. As we grew older, our imagination became more fragile with every shattered belief.

At some point the programming takes hold and replaces the belief in unlimited possibilities. We become so conditioned to accept the evidence of our current reality that we no longer believe in the power of our imagination. We write off things we aspired to do and never came to pass as "pipe dreams." Know this: the difference between imagining something and actually manifesting it lies in the depth of our belief that our future is dependent upon our current reality. Without imagination, nothing can change, but this must be coupled with the belief that whatever is in our imagination is just as real as that which we see evidence of in the physical world.

Nearly four centuries ago French philosopher and mathematician René Descartes wrote, "I think, therefore I am." People have been quoting him ever since, but how many really give thought to the meaning behind those words? Essentially, Descartes was saying that we are the energy of thought, manifested. We exist, and will continue to evolve, by virtue of our thoughts. Imagination is using the energy of thought to manifest everything.

Indeed, how does one plan for the future without it? We can imagine being on vacation sometime in the future and vividly picture it in our mind, even though our current reality tells us we are not on vacation. Yet we make these vacations a reality. Why then is creating a different life from the one we are currently living such an impossibility? The answer is, it isn't.

Just like we plan for our vacations in our imagination, we can imagine and create a different life. All it takes is envisioning it in our minds, then changing our thoughts and beliefs about the ability to make it our reality. It's really that simple.

What we think, we create. What we believe, we attract, and what we imagine, we become. *Without fail.*

Chapter Four

THE THREE ELEMENTS OF PURPOSE

he Three Elements of Purpose are *intention, expression and manifestation.* These are the *why* we do things, *how* we do them, and *what* is created. Just as we must be mindful of our thoughts, we must be mindful of what we do and how we are doing it. Though all three elements are important, intention is especially so. We must always ask ourselves, in all that we do, if what we are doing is serving our purpose.

Mindfulness is paying attention to your intention.

Intention

If someone asked you why you are reading this book, you would likely tell them it is because you want to find your purpose. *You have an intention.* Can you speak with such clarity about other things you do in your life? As is the case with our thoughts, we spend precious little time contemplating our actions. Most everything we do is out of habit; we never give much thought as to why we do it, or whether or not it serves our purpose.

As mentioned above, intention is the most important element of purpose, for it is with our intention that we can manipulate the energy and thus the circumstances of life. Mindfulness is nothing more than paying attention to our intention. Without mindfulness, we are living life by accident. However, when we set a clear intention to take some action (the expression of what we want to manifest), we take control of our own situation. We stop buying into the false idea of randomness.

Having intention is especially important when we're talking about our emotions. As we go through life, it often feels like our emotions are running us, when the truth is, just as we have total control over our thought, we also have the ability to control our emotions. However, without intention and mindfulness, we give away this control to circumstances and to other people, and we do this by reacting from emotion – be it frustration, anxiety, anger, et cetera. How do we change this? By using the energy of thought to create a buffer between ourselves and the external world.

Arguably, the greatest source of unhappiness is our belief that happiness is dependent upon circumstances. We tell ourselves that the external world needs to be exactly the way we want it in order for us to feel good. But how often does the world abide by this desire? Why does it rain when we made plans for some outdoor activity? Why does someone treat us in a way we find unacceptable? Why isn't our life going the way we want it to? Surely this is evidence that we can't create what we desire! If we look more closely at the situation, however, we will realize that we never set the intention of creating it in the first place. We also must consider that we are *co-creators*, with others and the Universe, and in this shared Universe we may not always get what we want, though we will get what we need. Knowing this, we must then decide to be okay regardless. In other words, we set the intention to be okay without requiring evidence of how or when it will manifest for us. We must trust the *process*.

Creating our life is analogous to ordering something online. When there is something we desire, we go to the website, place our order, and then trust it will arrive. We don't know exactly when it will be delivered, nor in what condition it will be in, but in ordering it we have triggered a chain of events that will result in its arrival. We have a similar process by which we create our life, but instead of a computer or a smart phone we use the three Elements of Mind and the Three Elements of Purpose. We place the order with the Universe and trust the process, believing our order will be fulfilled. This is true whether what we "order" is something we want or something we don't.

This is why we need to set clear intentions in everything we do, be mindful of these intentions to create the best possible means to manifest what we desire, and then let go of how or when it will happen and just *trust the process.*

Our shared, universal purpose is Love, uniquely and individually expressed as a manifestation of the Consciousness of the Universe.

Expression

Expression is the "how" of purpose, or the action we take to manifest it. Though we all share the same universal purpose, there are as many ways to express this purpose as there are people walking the earth. Remember, purpose is a process, and how we express it is where we put our imagination to use. It is what makes us unique and thus must be used in *everything we do,* no matter how big or small.

If our purpose is love, how do we express it? We start by loving ourselves, just as we are. To do this, we must develop a deep understanding and awareness of the relationship we have with our own self.

If we can learn to love ourselves, everything else falls into place. When we love our self, we take care of all aspects of our being, and this allows us to express love in all we manifest. The food we make, the chores we do around the house, the jobs we do, the relationships we create, et cetera — everything becomes an opportunity to manifest our purpose.

We are the manifestation of the Consciousness of the Universe, co-creating and manifesting our life into existence.

Manifestation

Manifestation is nothing but thought, belief and imagination put into action that results in the creation of something. It is what appears in our physical reality when we use the energy within the Elements of the Mind. It is a very simple concept to grasp. We are a manifestation of the Consciousness of the Universe (or God). It created our Earth and everything on it, including us. Similarly, every single thing humans have ever created is a manifestation of thought, belief and imagination, applied to purpose.

Whether you realize it or not, you have manifested everything in your life, from the simple things like what you ate for dinner to the relationships you have, your children, your career, et cetera — none of which existed beforehand. You may have done it without intention, but you have done it just the same, so why is it so difficult to believe that you can manifest anything you wish to have in your life?

Remember, though, that you can't manifest something that doesn't currently exist without the thought to create it, the belief that you can create it, and the trust that it will arrive. Using the foundational Elements of the Mind, we create everything.

There are a plethora of books and movies on the Law of Attraction, all of which teach that we can manifest anything we desire. If we want a new house, car or boat, a dream vacation, et cetera, we can have it, even if in our current reality it seems completely out of reach. There are various theories about the amount of action, if any, is needed; that said, I will explore later in this book how the Law of Attraction works for us when we are both aligned with the Universe and clear in our intentions about what we wish to attract.

Our focus right now, however, is *life* itself and *what we want our life to become,* outside of the material. We can't buy health, happiness, satisfying careers, great relationships, or knowledge and understanding. If we cannot buy them (like we would a new car), then how do we manifest them? Most believe that having these things is just a matter of random luck, which is just another faulty belief.

We don't buy a great life, we create it! If we want good health, we create it through the Three Elements of Mind and then, using the Three Elements of Purpose, we set the intention and express it by taking action (i.e. a healthy diet and exercise) which then manifests good health. If we want a satisfying career, we imagine doing what we love and take action to create a career from that. If we want great relationships, we first create a great relationship with our self, and then as we love ourselves we are also able to express that love in our interaction with others. We *create* the life we want by using and manipulating energy. If we put as much effort into creating the life we want as we did into acquiring material things, we could easily be living it.

This may surprise you, but just as we will never be satisfied with the chasing and acquiring of material possessions, we can never be fully satisfied by chasing after our purpose as if it too were a singular thing. Think about it. Oftentimes we pursue a material object because we believe it will bring us happiness. We go through the steps, consciously or un-consciously, of manifesting that object, only to find that the feeling of satisfaction quickly passes and true happiness continues to elude us. If we haven't learned our lesson by then (that true contentment cannot be found in the physical world), we're soon off chasing after something else in order to be happy. The same is true if we limit our purpose to one particular thing (i.e. a career that fulfills us); eventually we realize something is missing and the search will be on again. This is why purpose is not a thing we seek, but a process of *living*. Remember, life is energy itself. Manifestation is creation. Purpose is the process of creating our life. When we fail to trust the process, it creates conflict, and conflict is something we must learn to resolve.

Chapter Five

THE TWO ELEMENTS
OF MEANING

Our experience creates conflict and through its resolution we achieve growth, which provides contextual meaning for our life.

There are two elements we struggle with that give our life meaning: conflict and the resolution of that conflict. Typically when we think of conflict it is as an argument or dispute between or amongst people, countries, and so on. But for our purposes here, however, conflict is defined as some kind of disturbance in our energy, whether the stimuli are external or internal (i.e. between our ego and our spirit). In fact, while both external and internal stimuli can cause this disturbance we feel, *all conflict is actually internal.*

From our singular vantage point we can see the world as being very different from the way we wish it would be. So long as the world and everyone in it is exactly the way we want it, we feel no disturbance within. Whenever something is not the way we want it or someone is not behaving the way we want them to, it causes internal conflict. This is why, in the lower levels of purpose, we tend to place the blame for our struggle in life onto something or someone else. When we realize, however, that we can change neither the external world nor other people, we understand that the only way to resolve this conflict is by changing our own thinking. Because life exists entirely within our mind, until we come to realize that all our conflict is within, we cannot fully resolve it.

Life is continual conflict. It is in the resolution of it that gives us contextual meaning, and this is how we experience life and grow. Every decision we make is born out of conflict, from the simple to the complex. Let's consider some scenarios that illustrate how continual conflict plays out in our life.

The alarm clock goes off, waking us up and introducing conflict. *"Should I hit the snooze button or get up?"* Either way, once we do get out of bed we are faced with another decision — *"Should I get dressed or make coffee first?"* — and hence more conflict. We're late for work — more conflict. Stop lights, traffic jams, dealing with other drivers — more conflict. And that's just the trivial stuff. What about, *"Should I change careers? Get married? Have children? Seek my purpose in life?"* — all conflict needing resolution. Every person we meet and every situation we find ourselves in introduces conflict. Try as we might, there is no avoiding it; it is *everywhere, all the time.*

Think of how someone says or does something that causes a disturbance within us. As much as we would like to blame them for this disturbance, what's really happening is this person is not behaving the way we want them to and so it introduces internal conflict. Most often, our reaction is an attempt to correct the other person to be in alignment with our own expectations of them. Yet because we cannot change another, the problem lies not in *their* behavior but in our own inner conflict that we avoid dealing with. Until we learn to master and resolve this conflict within us, these situations will repeat over and over again until we learn from them and are able to let them go and move on.

What we believe, we attract. So long as we keep believing our problems lie in others, we will keep attracting them and the same behaviors until we learn to resolve the conflict within. Once we master this, we will see that we no longer attract these conflicts. The next time a similar behavior from another (external stimuli) presents itself, it will no longer cause us conflict because we have already learned the lesson and how to instantly resolve it. We may still attract these people and situations, but not the conflict that goes along with them.

As strange as it may sound, conflict is not only good for us, but a necessary element of living with purpose. Avoiding conflict will not bring us peace; only the *resolution of conflict* does that. So embrace your conflict and grow or avoid it and remain stuck in it. The choice is always yours.

When I was a child, I saw beauty in everything and everyone around me. I tried in vain to show this beauty to others. Why couldn't they see it for themselves? I felt misunderstood and like an outcast, as if this beauty was all in my head. I also believed they thought I was crazy for seeing something that didn't exist. This conflict lowered my energy and because I avoided it, it manifested in my life as frustration, anger and depression. I also suffered and struggled with various addictions and a very unhealthy, if not dangerous, lifestyle. In other words, I was a mess. However, when I learned to resolve the conflict and love myself, I raised my energy, and it became clear that my purpose was to inspire and show others the beauty within themselves and the world around them. This is why I became an artist, musician, writer and life coach. All it took was embracing the conflict and resolving it, and my life changed *dramatically*.

It is in our greatest struggle, our deepest pain, and the greatest source of conflict that our purpose lies. Once we resolve it, we will have discovered where we need to express our purpose. This is how we can best be in service to others. Look deep within yourself. What is your greatest source of pain? What do you struggle with the most? What causes you the greatest conflict? This is life showing you your purpose, but you will not recognize it as such as long as you see conflict as a problem to avoid rather than a lesson to be learned. Avoiding conflict will only make your purpose more elusive. Embracing and resolving conflict draws your purpose close.

To illustrate this I offer the story of a high school friend whose life completely turned around as a result of his decision to resolve his greatest conflict. For much of his life he was overweight, which was a source of pain and struggle and a symptom of his inability to overcome the conflict of abuse, abandonment and a lack of self-love. Once he learned to resolve the source of this conflict, conquer his pain and love himself, he then set out to fulfill his purpose by teaching others how to overcome and resolve the same issues. Today, he is a leader in the physical fitness and wellness fields.

Many of our greatest thinkers, teachers and most successful people took their pain and struggle and turned it into their greatest achievement. You can do the same thing. If you are not sure of your purpose, look to conflict for the answer. Embrace it and find a way to resolve it and your purpose will be revealed to you.

For a look at a common, albeit minor, external source of conflict, let's return to our rainy day example. You've made and are looking forward to outdoor plans, only to have them canceled when the heavens open up. This causes conflict. You can blame the rain for ruining your day, when the simple truth is it needs to rain in order to water all the plants and animals that live outdoors. The rain itself is not the source of the conflict; rather, the conflict lies within you.

You decided how the world needs to be for you to be okay. On this day, you needed it to *not rain.* That was your expectation. It is *you* who does not want it to rain because *you* made outdoor plans. Therefore, the conflict is not the fault of the rain, it's your own internal conflict because you believe your happiness depends on carrying out your plans. Resolve the internal conflict over *how you feel* about your plans being ruined, and you will have learned a valuable lesson that allows you to grow and find greater meaning. Learn the lesson, and the next time it rains on your outdoor plans you will allow it to just be what it is, without the conflict.

The energy that creates the rain is the same energy within you. You can block this energy by avoiding it (the conflict), or you can just allow it to flow through you (resolve it) and let it go. Everything in life, and every conflict we face plays out in a similar fashion and we alone have the power to remove the struggle by understanding our energy and how it works.

We can think of life as a hot air balloon. The energy resides within the balloon itself, just waiting to take off if we will allow it. Our bodies sit in the basket and we wish to soar above the clouds. Conflict can be thought of as the weights tied to our hot air balloon, preventing us from leaving the ground and soaring where we wish to go. Some of the weights are light and some are very heavy. They are also tied to different lengths of rope. So long as we avoid cutting ties with them, we will remain where we are, stuck on the ground. But if we start to resolve them, starting with the easiest, we will notice we feel lighter, and we're beginning to rise a little higher. It is the heaviest weights (conflicts) that hold us back the most, and when we deal with and resolve them, there is no limit to how high we can soar. As we rise above, our perspective changes and we gradually see the bigger picture of life until this vision we've only held in our imagination becomes real and fully manifested.

Ironically, one of the biggest weights that hold us back is the *lack* of something: love for ourselves. Like so many of our other beliefs, a lack of self-love has been programmed into us. When we rely only on physical evidence to support our thinking and beliefs, we can have a hard time loving ourselves and the life we live. Every conflict or unhappiness can ultimately be traced back to a lack of Love. However, when we learn to rise above those programmed beliefs to love ourselves and think and act out of Love, much of what caused the conflict magically disappears. It truly is amazingly powerful energy.

Love does not place conditions on anything or anyone. It is a lack of Love that causes us to create expectations of others and the world around us, and when these expectations are unfulfilled, we withhold Love. We then hate ourselves and/or others. We curse the rain. We're also moving away from our purpose rather than fulfilling it.

To recap, if we wish to discover and fulfill our purpose, we must embrace conflict, for it is in resolving it that we grow and derive meaning for our life. This keeps raising our energy and the more conflict we resolve the higher our energy soars. This is how we change ourselves and thus change the world around us.

Our purpose lies in our deepest pain, our greatest struggle. Embrace this conflict. Resolve it. Learn to love that part of your life you have hated for so long and your purpose will reveal itself to you.

Chapter Six

THE SIX ELEMENTS OF LIFE

The Six Elements of Life are the external elements of our purpose to which we direct our intention. They are our jobs or career, our finances, our physical and mental health, our relationships, our spirituality and our personal growth. The amount of intention we direct our purpose towards in these categories greatly affects how life plays out for us. Let's explore these elements to assess where we are and where we wish to be.

We weren't born merely to support our existence. There is indeed so much more to living than earning it. Attempts to escape or distract ourselves from it isn't living either.

Career

If there is one defining external element of purpose (or rather what we've come to define as purpose), it is our career. Everything we've been programmed and prepared for our entire life is about our profession.

Have you ever noticed just how much we identify ourselves by our job? When we are introduced to someone new, we first ask their name, and immediately follow it up with, "What do you do?" meaning what they do to make a living. We truly have a preoccupation with our occupation!

It perhaps comes as no surprise that we give so much importance to our career, as we will spend roughly one-third of our life devoted to it. It's easy to see, then, why we can confuse profession with purpose, and to feel like we have missed the boat with regard to purpose when we are spending so much time and energy in a profession that we find no satisfaction in.

We've been taught that when we grow up we need to earn a living, not only to support ourselves and our families, but to make as much money as we can so we can afford to buy material possessions and, presumably, our happiness. We spend our youth and middle age striving to pay for vacations and material possessions, all the while hoping we'll be able to save enough over our lifetime to be able to retire, so we can *then* do what we want with our life. Unfortunately, by then, we only have a relatively short time left to enjoy it.

Why do we do this? Once again, it is our programming. Some, as mentioned above, confuse profession with purpose, some believe that earning a living and living your purpose are mutually exclusive. We believe these falsehoods even when we may *earn more money by fulfilling our purpose.*

Some people do find a career, intentionally or unintentionally, that aligns with their dreams or passion, but most do not. Most just believe that we are what we do, and a good portion of them will end up becoming very dissatisfied beings, essentially hating one-third of their lives.

Even those who began their journey with great plans of doing something they love oftentimes wind up giving up on it to settle for a job that pays the bills. Sadly, this often results in trying to escape our life rather than living it. We find escapes in hobbies, weekend reprieves, vacations and dreams of retirement. When those do not suffice, we distract ourselves from this unfulfilling life we've created by dulling our senses with drugs, alcohol or other addictive or toxic behavior. Anything that helps us avoid dealing with the fact that we've lost our purpose seems easier than trying to fulfill it.

While our profession is not synonymous with purpose, it is arguably the best gauge of the level of purpose from which we are currently operating. It shows where we are devoting a large portion of our time, and whether we wish to be rewarded with more than a paycheck. That said, we are taught to judge our level of professional fulfillment by how much money we earn when in fact they are two separate topics. I will discuss finances in the next section.

Indeed, it is possible to create a career out of doing what we love. This leads us back to the common notion of purpose, that if we could only do what we love, we will then be forever happy. This too is programmed thinking. A satisfying career is certainly worth pursuing, but if we are to truly understand that purpose is not a thing to seek but a process of how we experience life, we can fulfill our purpose by learning to love whatever we do, no matter what that is. Again, the key is Love. Hating any aspect of our life is essentially hating ourselves. Loving ourselves is part of our purpose. When we love our self, we will find a way to pursue that which reflects this Love and no one and nothing will be able to stop us from doing so.

Money is not the root of all evil.
It's the love of money that is the root of evil.
The love of money is greed.

Finances

First, we must understand that there really is nothing inherently wrong with money. Money is an inanimate object and more an illusion than a reality. Yes, we need it to live, and the more money we have the more freedom we have. But in reality, money is nothing more than numbers on a computer that get moved around like a grand shell game. In essence, we are chasing after something that is constantly getting shifted from one person to another. Our idea about it is generally another falsehood we've adopted as our truth. We're not in love with money, but what it represents to us.

Money is not the root of all evil. It's the love of it, or greed, that can cause us to act in an unethical or "evil" manner. But this is yet another illusion, and one that often leads to hypocrisy. We can simultaneously desire to acquire as much money as we possibly can for ourselves, yet also begrudge others who do the same. We can envy people who are rich, and also hate them for having riches. We certainly appreciate the money we receive for goods and services we provide to others but then we complain about the price of goods and services others provide us. When we have this kind of negative energy about money, we will always be in the energy of lack. We must stop believing this and instead be grateful for the abundance we can all share in.

The pursuit of money is not our purpose; it is a by-product of living with purpose. When we are not fulfilling our purpose whatever we do to earn money can feel like drudgery that drains our energy. Even if we acquire wealth, we end up always wanting more of it as a substitute for our lack of purpose. This is a very low level of energy to live in. The goal is to find a way to align our purpose with the goal of acquiring wealth so that neither our career nor finances are impediments to our growth.

Once we realize that our career and our finances are just two elements of many, we can reprioritize our life and pursue our purpose. Then, like everything else in our physical reality, our career and finances become reflections of this pursuit.

When we recognize that money is merely an exchange mechanism for things we want and need, we are able to release our programmed attachment to money itself, thus freeing us up to live with purpose without assigning a dollar amount to it. When our belief about money is aligned with our purpose, the money will come. This goes back to how our thoughts create and our beliefs attract. Believe in your purpose and you will attract the money as a simple by-product of that belief.

Just as with other areas of our life, we need to set intentions when it comes to our finances. This is not about being greedy or about feeling superior to others, but about attracting the money we need and desire as it aligns with our purpose. What we imagine we become, so if we can imagine becoming wealthy, we eventually will, but only if we have resolved our conflicts around it and take the steps to manifest it.

We are what we eat, and what we are as a society is overwhelmingly unhealthy. What we think we create, and what we think is largely what we feed our mind.

Health

The state of our physical and mental health is determined by the food we eat, the exercise we partake in and what we feed or program our subconscious mind with each day.

Health is an important element to our purpose. When we are unhealthy in body or mind, we cannot be happy or content. The state of our physical health greatly affects our mental health, just as our mental health affects our physical health. We cannot neglect one and expect the other to be healthy.

As mentioned earlier, the Law of Attraction requires trust and an expectation that what we desire will be delivered to us. That said, there is a difference between having an expectation and taking something for granted. We tend to think of health as a given, and illness being some random act of bad luck. We lack an understanding of what creates good health and, just as we don't actively live with purpose and create the life we desire, we don't actively participate in the creation of good health. In fact, it often seems as though we would rather trade it for temporary gratification.

The food we eat is mostly chosen to satisfy our hunger (or in reality, lust) because it tastes good and makes us feel happy in the moment. We call it "comfort food" for a reason. We knowingly eat food that is bad for our health, all the while telling ourselves we will do better "tomorrow" or "after the holidays." But tomorrow never comes, at least not until we've either become obese or severely ill. Even then, we still sometimes rationalize or justify eating poorly (i.e. "I had a bad day," or "I don't have time to cook," when the truth is if we truly loved ourselves, we would choose a healthy diet. A poor diet is a reflection of something we hate about ourselves, as well as an escape from an unfulfilling life.

Just as we are not mindful of what we subject our bodies to, we also feed our minds a lot of negative, unhealthy stimuli with no regard to its effect on us. Far too many immerse themselves in violent movies and video games, watch negative news, read and write negative social media posts and engage in a lot of complaining and negative self-talk. The end result is an unhealthy mindset which manifests an equally negative reality.

We cannot be mentally healthy when the mind is fed a steady diet of toxic fare.

Our mental and physical state will always reach some equilibrium. We can be physically strong but mentally weak, and eventually our physical state will weaken. Conversely, we can be mentally strong, but with prolonged illness or pain our mental state will deteriorate. To love ourselves is to seek good physical and mental health and be balanced in mind and body.

We must set the intention to become as mentally and physically healthy as we can be and then take action to make it so. It is within strong health that our purpose can be fulfilled.

Without a healthy mind and body, our purpose will always be limited.

Love your neighbor as yourself.

Relationships

Few things are as important to us as the connections we make with other people. However, when we do not place a high priority on self-love, our relationships with others will inevitably suffer, for we will always be looking to them for that which we are not providing ourselves.

Make a list of everyone you love. Now look at it. Are you on it? You should be, and you should be at the top of the list. Not many people put themselves on a list of people they love. That's our programming. We've been taught to sacrifice our self-love and put everyone else above our own well-being.

Obviously, we should care about others and even be in service to them, but we must first cultivate enough self-love to become the best possible version of ourselves. Anything less than our best not only undermines our purpose but short-changes the world of the great contributions we can make to it, not to mention what we can offer our families, friends, colleagues, and so on.

When we love ourselves, everything else we do is then fulfilling our purpose. Every single element of purpose is expressed through the Love we have for ourselves. When we love ourselves, we love our life and everything in it, including those we share our life with.

Nothing anyone says about or to us, or how they treat us, has anything to do with us. It has everything to do with how they see themselves and whether they love themselves or not. Likewise, everything you think about or say to another, and the way you treat them, is entirely because of how you feel about yourself.

When we love ourselves, we naturally attract strong, healthy relationships with others. When we love ourselves, we don't seek friendships that undermine or sabotage our purpose, but like-minded people who want to grow with us. When we love ourselves, we don't seek mates out of a need for them to complete us, because we are already complete just as we are. This allows us to love and be loved for the joy of it, without obligation or expectation. This is the definition of unconditional Love.

Nothing erodes a relationship more than expectations. Expectations that go unfulfilled lead to disharmony, jealousy, envy, frustration and even hatred. When we love ourselves and are fulfilling our purpose, then we do not expect others to fulfill it for us, thus those negative emotions are minimized if not eliminated altogether.

I am supremely confident in my beliefs,
for I know they must change.

Spirituality

We all have a connection to the energy of the Consciousness of the Universe. Some call that God, others call it Higher Power, or Source, Creator and so on. Whatever belief we hold is typically what we were taught by our parents. This could be a religion, or a philosophy about life, but no matter what our core values and beliefs are, they were ingrained in us at an early age and we typically cling to them for dear life, to the exclusion of any other ideas.

Of course, as we grow older and have more experiences with others who believe differently, and if we are open-minded enough, we might come to understand belief systems other than the one we were indoctrinated into. We may even begin to understand that in a Universe with billions of galaxies, each containing billions of stars with billions of other planets, how limited our perspective really is.

Spirituality is not the same as religion. As French philosopher and Jesuit priest Pierre Teilhard de Chardin once said, *"You are not a human being in search of a spiritual experience. You are a spiritual being immersed in a human experience."* If we can put aside our individual beliefs and embrace our spiritual nature, we can then see our purpose in a new way. It is our connection to the energy of the Consciousness of the Universe that allows us to fully use our imagination to visualize a different life for ourselves, and then use our thought to create it and our belief to attract it.

Whereas being religious usually means ascribing to a predetermined set of beliefs, being spiritual is more about lifting the burden of physical limitations off our shoulders, thereby freeing ourselves to pursue our purpose to its fullest potential. Our spirit is energy consciousness. When we are aware of this, we have no limitations. Anything is possible.

That said, we will have to contend with the ego, that place in which everything we've been programmed to believe resides. In fact, the ego can *only* believe what it has been programmed to believe, and it uses this programming, along with evidence of our present reality, to determine what is possible. It knows nothing else. Our spirit, on the other hand, is what allows us to imagine a different reality. This is the eternal nature of our spirit, the energy within us, or who we really are. When new information or understanding presents itself to us, the ego rebels, and this causes conflict.

As mentioned earlier, all conflict is internal and stems from a battle waged between our ego (the subconscious programmed mind) and our spiritual nature (the energy of thought and imagination). The ego is what causes us to "believe it when we see it," meaning we need proof. However, our spirit, using our beliefs, will attract the very things our ego sees no evidence of. In spirit, we will see it because we believe it to exist already.

Our experience creates conflict and through its resolution we achieve growth, which provides contextual meaning for our life.

Personal Growth

Since the day we were born, we've been "growing up." When we're little we're asked, "What do you want to be when you grow up?" When we are acting in an immature way, we are admonished to "Grow up!" We have this programmed idea that once we reach adulthood, we have "grown up," as if there is no further growth required. Nothing could be further from the truth.

Part of our purpose is the *process of growth*. This means that in order to fulfill our purpose, we must be in a continual state of growth. Everything we experience can give our life meaning, but only when we have learned some lesson within it. As mentioned earlier, life hands us lessons in the form of conflict. Without conflict we would lack awareness of the opportunity for growth. We feel content by resolving discontent. We feel happy by resolving that which makes us unhappy. Conflict is a necessary element of purpose because according to the Theory of Purpose, it is in the resolution of conflict that we derive meaning and grow.

Many of us stop seeking growth once we reach adulthood. We don't attempt to create new experiences, seek new opportunities, or learn new things about ourselves or the world we live in. Instead, we get into the routine of "maintaining" where we are. But we can take these elements of life and continually work at them, striving to be better tomorrow than we are today. This is the continual growth we can seek *on purpose.* We start by looking back at each element of our lives and assessing whether we are growing, or if we are just in "maintenance" mode.

Chapter Seven

THE FOUR LEVELS
OF PURPOSE

*E*ach and every one of us is already experiencing and fulfilling our purpose, even if we are unaware of doing so. The reason is that we all share a universal purpose, one that gives meaning to our existence far above any individual aspirations. That purpose is love.

However, while we are all fulfilling our purpose, we are not all operating on the same level. This is not a judgment (as if one level is better than another), but merely a statement of where each of us is on our journey. We all take different paths through these levels of purpose, with some staying longer on a given level than others. Our purpose can be expressed and experienced on any level, yet there is always room to grow and evolve, both within each level and in order to move to the next.

Thought (which we use to create), *belief* (which we use to attract), and *imagination* (which is what we become) is used to *manifest* and *express* our purpose via our *intention*. We grow and find meaning in these levels of purpose via the *resolution* of *conflict* that we experience in the Six Elements of Life (*Career, Finance, Health, Relationships, Spirituality,* and *Personal Growth*). This is the Theory of Purpose, using the elements that define it.

The Four Levels of Purpose are Material, Ego, Altruistic and Enlightened. We are born into the Material level. This is when our eternal spirit enters a body and thus becomes a physical manifestation of this world we live in. Because we are now both spiritual and physical beings, we will experience continual conflict between our ego and spirit. This is the internal struggle of life. The Six Elements of Life will present the external conflict of our struggle. Resolving these conflicts is how we experience life, by learning and growing in our purpose. As we grow in purpose, we move into higher levels of it. How far we get depends on how willing we are to change our thoughts and beliefs.

Let's explore each level of purpose, followed by the Six Elements of Life and how we typically deal with conflict.

The Material Purpose

Overview: We seek happiness in materialism. We spend our life acquiring enough wealth to provide not only financial stability, but the ability to afford the luxuries of life that we derive pleasure from.

The Six Elements of Life on the Material Level:

- **Career** — Our educational system and programming is all about obtaining the best job or career we can find. Job satisfaction or how it reflects our purpose is of little value.

- **Finance** — This level is all about money. It is what drives us. We find happiness in our material possessions, yet because this happiness is a baseless illusion, we are always left dissatisfied and wanting more.

- **Health** — On this level we take very little, if any, responsibility for our health. We believe drugs cure everything. Drug addiction is at its highest on this level. On this level we experience the highest levels of stress and develop many mental issues and disorders.

- **Relationships** — Our relationships, good and bad, are mostly based on a false sense of obligation. On this level we have almost no relationship with our own self, which leads us to seek the things we are missing (within ourselves) in others.

- **Spirituality** — On this level we are more religious than spiritual. Our beliefs, while deep and strong, are not expressed or manifested in our reality. Like our physical health, we absolve ourselves of our spiritual responsibility. Our beliefs (outside of religion) require evidence.

- **Personal Growth** — There is very little personal growth on this level. Most everything is superficial in nature as we present a façade to others in order to be accepted.
- **Conflict** — On this level conflict is mostly avoided unless we are forced to deal with it. We often blame someone or something else for what is wrong with our life, thus stunting our own growth.

The Ego Purpose

Overview: This is the level most associate with "purpose" because it is about "doing what we love" in keeping with the traditional thought that if we could only follow our passion and fulfill our dreams we would be happy and content.

The Six Elements of Life on the Ego Level:

- **Career** — This is the level where we seek to "do what we love" to satisfy the ego's desire to be recognized for our uniqueness.
- **Finance** — On this level we are more willing to take financial risks that align with our newfound purpose.
- **Health** — Because we have awakened, and desire to be more in tune with our purpose, we seek out more knowledge and understanding. On this level we take more responsibility for our health.
- **Relationships** — We are exploring ourselves in an attempt to find deeper meaning in life and are beginning to love ourselves more. Because of this, our relationships are less about obligation and more aligned with our purpose. Because we are exercising more self-care, we have more to give others in our relationships.

- **Spirituality** — On this level, we will discover more of our true nature and place less stock in our programming. We may remain religious, but we find ourselves being more open to coexisting with others whose beliefs are different from our own.
- **Personal Growth** — Because our thoughts and beliefs have changed, we are more open to growth. The more we grow, the more we desire it.
- **Conflict** — While we still spend far too much time and energy avoiding conflict, we find that this level creates more of it (both internally and externally), and so we begin developing more effective ways of resolving it.

The Altruistic Purpose

Overview: We find deeper meaning in being of service to others. We are no longer solely concerned with satisfying our personal need and desire to live with passion and purpose and seek to connect with and help others.

The Six Elements of Life on the Altruistic Level:

- **Career** — On this level we seek jobs or careers that are more in line with our goals of serving others. We also volunteer ourselves more to those in need.
- **Finance** — On this level we donate more money to worthwhile causes. While we still have a need for money and a desire to acquire more, we think in terms of what we can do with our money that makes a positive impact on the world.
- **Health** — Our focus is not on staving off illness, but on being the best we can be, both physically and mentally. We desire more knowledge about health and take far more responsibility for it.

- **Relationships** — On this level we have learned to be more discerning with our relationships, removing toxic people from our lives that do not serve our purpose. We seek more positive, like-minded people to share our lives with.
- **Spirituality** — On this level we seek a deeper connection with God, which requires a lot of inner work using the Three Elements of Mind. We seek a deeper connection with others as well.
- **Personal Growth** — This is the level where we seek the most growth. The more we understand ourselves and our place in the Universe, the more questions arise. Growth on this level happens from deeper transformative experiences.
- **Conflict** — We embrace conflict on this level because we seek growth, knowing it is in the resolution of conflict that gives contextual meaning to our existence.

The Enlightened Purpose

Overview: We seek a connection with God, thus fulfilling our greatest purpose and highest calling. We realize that life isn't about us at all, nor is it just about a connection with others; rather, it is about being in a continual state of connection with everything in the Universe where our self is dissolved into the whole.

The Six Elements of Life on the Enlightened Level:

- **Career** — When we become enlightened, what we do with our lives is viewed from a much larger perspective and so we do not fixate on our work. Satisfaction, joy and meaning comes from how we live and experience life, not from what we do to earn a living.

- **Finance** — When we are enlightened, money is seen as a means to an end, not the end itself. We no longer chase after material things because we know our possessions do not determine our level of happiness or contentment.
- **Health** — Our external (ego) and internal (spiritual) beings coexist in harmony. We have learned to integrate both into a consciousness of wellness.
- **Relationships** — We no longer see ourselves as separate from other living things, whether it is people, animals, plants, et cetera. We know we are connected to all life. This Love we have for ourselves is naturally extended to all living things, great and small. We lose judgment over others.
- **Spirituality** — We reside more in spirit than in ego. What ego we do have is completely under our control and viewed in a contextual manner. We realize that we are not only a manifestation of the Consciousness of the Universe (God), but the consciousness itself, expressed through our physical experience.
- **Personal Growth** — On this level we have transcended the entire idea of "personal" and instead know that our uniqueness is cause for separateness, not oneness. We see our self as a part of the whole of existence.
- **Conflict** — Conflict no longer exists. We see it for what it is, just another part of this illusion we've created to experience life.

Chapter Eight

OUR PURPOSE IS LOVE

*T*he power to create our life and fulfill our purpose lies in utilizing all Three Elements of Purpose at the same time so that each becomes integrated into the whole of our being. Love is what binds these elements together. When we think, believe, imagine and act out of Love in all that we do, this Love (our purpose) is expressed to its fullest. This is the Alchemy of Purpose. If we lack even a single element, we will experience conflict. However, when all of the elements are bound together in Love, we have no conflict; we have harmony, peace and joy. This is what we find in the Enlightened level of purpose.

The entire reason we exist is to love ourselves completely, and then express that Love towards all other life. This expression is the purpose that has been eluding so many of us.

The energy of Love is pure; one cannot love unconditionally and hold anger, worry, fear, anxiety or guilt at the same time. We may think we love unconditionally, but more often than not we think "I will love you if (fill in the condition)," or "I will love myself if (fill in the condition)." This is a result of the programming of faulty thoughts and beliefs about what Love really is. Even when it comes to our family or others closest to us, we oftentimes feel obligation, which, whether we realize it or not, is a condition. Or, we may feel obligated to love people who, if given the choice, we never would have chosen to be in our life. This kind of Love always comes with expectations, many if not most of which go unfulfilled.

We do love our children unconditionally for the most part, at least when they are very young and innocent, before we program them. But as they grow up they begin to resist the programs we feed them, which leads to a lot of negative energy. Then the conditions of our love begin to surface. We withhold Love when they fail to meet our conditions, don't follow our rules, behave in a manner that tests our patience, if not our authority, and we then have emotional reactions that express anything but Love. This doesn't mean we don't love them, or love them less, but it does prove that our ability to show Love has its limitations.

We are happy with, and love people, so long as they meet the condition of not disturbing our energy. The minute they disturb our energy, Love disappears, even if only briefly. It's a part of the programming we hold. As mentioned earlier, we may very well love others and believe it is unconditional, but upon closer examination we can almost always find some condition, however subtle, that we've attached to it. We do this with everyone in our lives, always withholding Love until the condition is met.

This includes how we love ourselves. If we have an unfulfilling job or career, it isn't the job itself we hate. We hate ourselves for having to do it and we will keep withholding Love from ourselves until we find a rewarding career. If we are overweight, we don't hate being overweight. We hate ourselves for being overweight and will continue to withhold Love until we lose the weight. Anything we are not happy with is nothing more than a programmed condition we place on self-Love. As the relationships we have with others are based solely on the relationship we have with our self, we then look to them to fill that lack of Love, thereby placing conditions on them. And when they fail to meet those conditions, we withhold Love from them as well.

When we love ourselves fully there is no void to fill, thus no need to place conditions on another. This allows us to have healthy, loving relationships with others without the need for them to meet our expectations before we express Love to them. When we love ourselves without conditions, we no longer feel undeserving of great wealth, health, loving relationships or rewarding careers. Love for ourselves and others gives us the context from which to appreciate and love life itself.

We can learn much about unconditional Love from nature. We see the beauty in a gorgeous sunset and feel Love for it and are inspired. But there is also beauty in a weed that grows in our garden. Many do not see this, and they do not love that weed. They do not realize that the same atoms that make up the sunset also reside in that weed, and within all things in the Universe, including ourselves. This is Love, the interconnection of the Universe. When we see ugliness in that weed, we are looking at our own ugliness. When we learn to see beauty in all things, including those we consider "ugly," we will have found Love. There is beauty in our happiness, obviously, but when we see beauty in our struggle, we will then recognize Love, and in Love our purpose can be expressed, which will resolve the struggle.

Love eliminates conflict. Every single time. Look at every struggle you have, and you will find that Love is the answer. When we love ourselves, we express it by caring for our health, working in careers that express Love, creating and maintaining strong relationships, and so on.

When we love ourselves, live in Love, think in Love, imagine from a place of Love and act out of Love, the more our purpose is revealed and expressed. Then it doesn't matter what we do, because every thought, action and situation is an opportunity to experience and express Love. Just as thought is energy and life is energy, so is Love. In fact, Love is the most positive energy there is, and the root of every positive emotion we have.

Whether we realize it or not, anything we seek to change in our lives is because it is not expressing Love. When we are not happy in our career it is because we are not able to express Love through it. We become ill when we stop loving ourselves because Love requires us to nurture and care for our bodies. As seen above, every problem we have in any relationship, including the one with our self, stems from conditions we place on Love. Every negative emotion we hold exists due to a lack of Love.

Our life is defined and experienced by the amount of Love we have and express. We are Love itself, yet we are contained and controlled within the walls of an illusory world of our own creation; in other words, the physical world we manifest. Our beliefs in this illusory world are the cause of our unrest and desire for change; the stronger our belief in the illusion, the harder it is for us to break free from what holds us back.

We seek purpose much like we seek everything else in life, as if it were a remedy for something wrong rather than a way of being. Purpose can be elusive because it is Love itself and resides within us; therefore, it cannot be sensed in any physical manner (in the external world) without it first being sensed within. We can only be it. Therefore, purpose is a process of experiential growth. As we grow in Love, we rise through the levels of purpose, each increasingly stronger in Love. We become enlightened beings when we fully express Love in all that we do. Look deeply into every element of the Theory of Purpose and find Love within them. In the Three Elements of Mind you will be living in purpose by having loving thoughts, believing in Love, and imagining a world of Love. In the Three Elements of Purpose, we can manifest and express Love, with Love being our sole intention. In the Six Elements of Life we can love what we do, love sharing what we have, love having good health, loving ourselves and others, being Love in spirit and continually growing in Love. We can use Love to resolve our conflicts and become stronger in Love as we grow into the levels of purpose. Love is our purpose.

Imagine if you were Love itself.

If only you believed that.

The thoughts you would have.

The actions you would take.

The way you would treat yourself and others.

The things and people you would attract.

What you could become and the life you would have.

If only you would remember who you are.

You are Love itself.

Chapter Nine

PURPOSE INVENTORY EVALUATION

*I*f we wish to fully experience life and fulfill our highest purpose, we must first establish where we are, right now in this current moment, and see what changes need to be made in order to create our life the way we want it.

We have thus far explored all the elements of the Theory of Purpose. This aids us in understanding our currently held thoughts and beliefs regarding our purpose.

What level of purpose do you think you are currently manifesting? Below is the *Purpose Inventory Evaluation,* which explores how we use the Three Elements of Purpose as it pertains to the Six Elements of Life.

Before beginning the evaluation, I want you to go back to pages 36-46 and look through the description of each element; then come back here and rate their importance on a scale of 1 to 5 (with 5 being the most important and 1 the least important). Any life element can share equal importance with another. You are not prioritizing them here, but merely assessing which life elements you think are most important to you right now.

Then, after you've rated them, fill in the area under each of the Six Elements of Life, where it shows the Three Elements of Purpose - Manifestation: *What* you are doing in this area of life;

Expression: *How* you are working on it; and Intention: *Why* you are working on it. Describe them as best you can. The last thing you need to contemplate is conflict. Describe your greatest struggle or most difficult conflict you are facing in each of those life elements. For example, under Career your struggle might be in finding the career of your dreams, or simply to find a job to support yourself. In Finance, you might be wanting security so you can retire, struggling to make ends meet, or longing to become wealthy. Under Health, you may be facing a severe illness, or you may just need to lose weight. Under Relationships, you might be going through a divorce or dealing with an abusive spouse, or still dealing with long-held problems with your parents. Under Spirituality you might be questioning your faith or struggling with the meaning of life. Whatever you struggle with, big or small, identify it as something you wish to work on.

Career —
>   **What** am I doing with this part of my life?
>   **How** am I working on it?
>   **Why** am I doing it?
>   **Conflict:** What am I struggling with in this element?

Finance —
>   **What** am I doing with this part of my life?
>   **How** am I working on it?
>   **Why** am I doing it?
>   **Conflict:** What am I struggling with in this element?

Health —
>   **What** am I doing with this part of my life?
>   **How** am I working on it?
>   **Why** am I doing it?

    Conflict: What am I struggling with in this element?

Relationships —

    What am I doing with this part of my life?

    How am I working on it?

    Why am I doing it?

    Conflict: What am I struggling with in this element?

Spirituality —

    What am I doing with this part of my life?

    How am I working on it?

    Why am I doing it?

    Conflict: What am I struggling with in this element?

Personal Growth —

    What am I doing with this part of my life?

    How am I working on it?

    Why am I doing it?

    Conflict: What am I struggling with in this element?

Next, I want you to revisit pages 49-53, where I discuss how the Six Elements of Life intersect with the Four Levels of Purpose and determine which one you most resonate with. Which level of purpose do you feel you are fulfilling at this very moment? I want you to think deeply about this and honestly evaluate how you are currently living your life. There is no right or wrong answer, and you might find yourself in between levels. Do not think in terms of where you want to be just yet, just focus on the now. We can't know where to go or how to get there if we are not aware of where we are presently.

Results and Analysis

So, at which level are you currently operating? Did you find it difficult to see yourself on a particular level? If so, you're not alone. Many find it hard to objectively see themselves as being on a particular level. Others might recognize features of one level they can see in themselves, but overall are unsure of where they really are. Most see features of all levels that might exist in their life, but upon closer inspection they realize it is more a desire to be that way than how they are truly living. If you aren't sure, go back to pages 49-53 and reread the explanation of each level. Having the desire to live on a particular level is a great starting point, but you must be honest in your assessment. This is not a judgement call, but an exercise to gauge where you really are so that you can find your way moving forward.

Be sure to save your answers to the evaluation, because when you are done reading this book, I'll ask you to go back and reevaluate them. Hopefully you will see what you must work on in order to raise your level of purpose, achieve all you can in life, and find deep, lasting meaning and fulfillment in it.

Evaluating where we are in the current moment is only part of the equation. In order to get to where we want to go and become what we wish to be, we must, first and foremost, understand ourselves. We need to explore *who we are*.

Chapter Ten

WHO ARE YOU?

"Who am I and why am I here?" These are two of the most profound questions we humans could ever ask ourselves. When we have found the answer to the first question, the answer to the second becomes apparent; however, in terms of life purpose it is not quite that simple. Why? Because the depth of our answer to the first question, "Who am I?" is dependent upon how deeply we explore the question itself. In our search to answer that eternal question, we will find that it (like our purpose) is a lengthy process, a journey of discovery we are not always ready to embark on.

From the moment of our birth we were given labels and had our identity shaped by others, all without our input. We just accepted it because we didn't know any different. We were given a name, and whether we were called Bob, Sally or whatever, we never were, nor will we ever be, our name. It is an identifier, but not our identity. I identify myself as Mark, and yet this does not begin to scratch the surface of who I am. As mentioned earlier, when introduced to others it is commonplace to ask (and be asked) what we do for a living. This is another identifier, and also not who we really are. I'm a writer, an artist, a musician, a father, husband, brother, son, et cetera, but while these things are (important) aspects of me, they are not who I really am at my core.

Labels we use to establish our identity are extremely entrenched in the programming of the Material level. We desperately want to belong, and in our desire for acceptance we blindly accept the labels given to us. We can even be arrogant with our labels because some can give us a sense of power, self-worth, value, and self-righteousness. It is not surprising, then, that being stripped of these self-important labels can make us feel like the world is crashing down around us. We can also be labeled with criticism and negative judgment and accept it, thereby damaging our well-being. This is only when we lack awareness of who we really are.

Over the years we were given various labels – child, teenager, adolescent, or adult – yet again, none of these things were who we really are. We were always an eternal being, simply going through the stages of human development. And yet we internalized these labels and had a love/hate relationship with them, which has caused us conflict. The most difficult years were those when we were labeled teenagers, when we no longer were as carefree as children and not yet as independent as adults. We also, during this period, lacked awareness of who we truly are, which made for plenty of conflict.

For many, it doesn't get any easier when we become adults; in fact it may even become more difficult. By then, we have lost the ability to separate who we are from the labels we identify with. These labels can be positive or negative; they can be ones we give ourselves or those given us by others. They can also be a source of great conflict.

Labels can be about what we do, or how we see ourselves based on our current reality. We *are* healthy or sick; we *are* rich or poor; we *are* happy or depressed; we *are* anxious; we *are* worried we *are* fearful, et cetera. Within our imagination we can become our labels, and so long as we hold them as our truth change is difficult, if not impossible. We may even take offense to any criticism of a label, because we identify with it so strongly.

We seek the truth of who we are, yet some spend their entire life without really knowing themselves. These people remain in the purgatory of Materialism, always identifying themselves by their labels. Others change their labels like chameleons, becoming one thing or another just to fit in.

If we discover our "purpose" and "do what we love," is this who we then become? What do you wish to become? Is that then who you are? If we define ourselves by *what* we do, who are we when we're not doing it? Know that *what* we become is not *who* we become; know that *whatever we do* with our life, this is not who we are. Who we are is eternal; it is not subject to the judgment of others, or ourselves. This begs the question, if you stripped away every single identifying label used to describe who you are, what would you be left with?

The Theory of Purpose provides a clue: *"We are the manifestation of the Consciousness of the Universe, co-creating and manifesting our life into existence."* But what does this mean at the individual level?

We can start to know ourselves by understanding what we are not; for example, as discussed above, we are not the external labels assigned to us by others. Clinging to these labels is an act of the ego, of wanting to be unique, when in fact who we really are is universally the same. When we cling to a belief that causes separateness it actually blinds us to the truth we are seeking.

We are also not our physical bodies. Contemplating our connection to others can help us understand this. For example, when we read books, we feel a connection with the author. We allow the writer into our mind, even though the writer isn't there with us and may not even be alive. We know another human being is communicating with us, stirring thought or emotion within us, yet their physical presence isn't required. We can see a work of art and it moves us, but the artist need not be there for us to feel what the artist felt while creating it. Music stirs our emotions whether we're listening to it live or on a radio or other device. The eternal connection we feel with other human beings transcends the limitations of this world, including our individual backgrounds, circumstances and physical forms.

We are not our thoughts, beliefs or imagination either. They reside in the mind and are just the tools we use to express who we are — a being that existed long before we got programmed with all these labels, false identities and misguided beliefs. Thus, in order to figure out who we are, we must strip away the programming, like peeling back the layers of an onion, to reveal what is underneath: the I AM.

As the I AM, we are creators of our life. We are artists. But where does this artist within reside? Within the body, the brain, the mind? It is in asking ourselves these questions that we will begin to understand who we truly are and what we want at the core level, rather than what we or others think we should be or want. This awareness, once discovered, can never be hidden away from us again. It is the *"what is once seen cannot be unseen."*

Take some time out of every day to just be alone with yourself and contemplate those two eternal questions: Who am I? Why am I here?

The answers are always found within, but *how* do we find this self-knowledge, this awareness of who we really are? Let's start at the beginning.

Chapter Eleven

IN THE BEGINNING

In science we call it "energy." In religion we call it our "soul." On the streets, we call it a "vibe." It's really all the same thing.

The very essence of who we are is our spirit. This oneness (interconnectedness with one another), and the ability to transcend physical boundaries with the energy of our thought, beliefs and imagination, lies in the very seat of our consciousness. We are spiritual beings of energy living in a physical world. It is this spiritual being we must get to know and understand if we are to create our life with purpose.

Since the beginning of time theologians and scientists alike have sought out the source of our being. While on the surface it appears these groups could not be more different, yet they share this singular, universal purpose we all must fulfill. Let's explore how they do this, using the Three Elements of Purpose (Manifestation or "what", Expression, or "how", and Intention, or "why").

What are they doing? They are doing something they have a passion for: exploration. Exploration is the manifestation.

How are they doing it? They became ministers, rabbis, shamans, yogis, et cetera, or they became geologists, astronomers or astrophysicists, et cetera. This is their unique expression of their purpose.

Why are they doing it? This is their intention. Religious leaders want to find the Creator (God). Scientists want to find the Source of Creation, and they ask whether it is God, or something else. While their purpose is expressed differently, in their intention they are living the same purpose.

I specifically chose scientists and religious leaders as examples because, really, they are both dealing with the same thing, energy. Whether we are talking about God creating the Universe, or the Big Bang, or how giant gas clouds condense into stars, or the Holy Spirit, everything that life is made of is energy. It lives in us and flows through us. It is what created us and what we use to create. It's all the same thing, just manifested into different physical objects.

Everything in the physical Universe, including us, is energy manifested by the Consciousness of the Universe, or God, and exists solely for the purpose of experiencing life. The experience itself is entirely within our mind, and how we experience it is a matter of choice. In other words, we choose how we use the energy within the elements of purpose.

If we are going to understand this spiritual being we are, there is just no getting around the discussion of God. Religion (or spirituality) and science need not be mutually exclusive. We all have our own beliefs, and all are valid and worthwhile so long as they serve our purpose. Once we become aware of and rise above our programming, the veil is lifted and the truth is revealed. There is no going back. There is still much of life to explore, but it will be done from a new awareness of our being.

We must have some existential reason for purpose. The Theory of Purpose demands it as we need something solid with which to build our life upon. While I was programmed at an early age into the teachings of Christianity, specifically as a

Protestant Lutheran, my spiritual foundation is Taoism. This has become my truth, but it will not necessarily be yours.

For you, the foundation may be Buddhism, Hinduism, Islam, Christianity, Paganism, or even Science. It doesn't really matter what our foundation is built of, so long as we have something underlying our purpose. Without that foundation, our purpose *has no purpose* other than selfish motivation, thus our intention will hold us in lower energy and the lower levels of purpose.

In the Taoist philosophy God is referred to as "That which cannot be named," or "That which is nameless." Any name or definition of God would limit God *in our mind*. Other groups refer to Source, the Creator, the Energy, the Consciousness of the Universe and so on. In Science, the living energy of the Universe that connects us all together might be explained by *string theory,* which in essence is the idea that everything is connected and only our perception sees separation. Even atheists can believe that there is something beyond the individual self, for example, "humanity's collective energy." Again, it doesn't matter how we label our beliefs; what's important is our understanding that who we are, why we are here, and our purpose cannot be described individually. Our universal purpose is entangled.

My use of the word "God" is meant to be inclusive of everyone. For the sake of discussion, we must give this "something beyond our self" a name, though, in the words of Shakespeare, "A rose by any other name would smell as sweet."

Our spirit is the most important component in creating our life, so whether you are a person of faith or of no faith at all, just realize that I am talking about being a part of the greater energy of Oneness that holds the Universe together, keeps it in motion and connects us all. This energy always was, is and always will be available to use, because we too *are* that energy. We are energy, manifested in the form of a human being, but *energy is what we are.* Love is energy.

As a manifestation of God, we carry within us all the power, talent, creativity, potential and energy to create our lives. As some might say, we are all made up of the same stardust as everything else in the Universe. That is powerful stuff!

Trust that you have this power or energy within you and know that you are a limitless being, capable of anything. The only thing holding you back is the limitation within your imagination.

Why then do we have such limited thinking in the first place and where does that come from? The answer is our ego, and more specifically how our ego has been programmed.

Chapter Twelve

THE EGO –
OUR PROGRAMMED REALITY

"The conscious and intelligent manipulation of the organized habits and opinions of the masses is an important element in democratic society. Those who manipulate this unseen mechanism of society constitute an invisible government which is the true ruling power of our country. We are governed, our minds are molded, our tastes formed, our ideas suggested, largely by men we have never heard of. This is a logical result of the way in which our democratic society is organized. Vast numbers of human beings must cooperate in this manner if they are to live together as a smoothly functioning society. In almost every act of our daily lives, whether in the sphere of politics or business, in our social conduct or our ethical thinking, we are dominated by the relatively small number of persons...who understand the mental processes and social patterns of the masses. It is they who pull the wires which control the public mind."

*T*he preceding quote is from Edward Bernays, author of the 1928 book, *Propaganda*. Bernays, who was the nephew of Sigmund Freud, is often referred to as the "father of public relations." He understood the human mind and how to manipulate it, and after emigrating to the United States from his native Austria he taught our government and corporations how to market their ideas and products to the general public. He did this by conditioning us to believe certain things, think in a particular way, and aspire to live in a certain manner.

Imagine what your life would be like if you had to discover the truth about yourself and the world around you on your own. Imagine if you had to rely on observation, experience, and self-exploration, instead of having your mind manipulated into thinking and believing the things you do. How different would your life be?

As we've discussed throughout this book, this is not the case. Our parents, society, religious institutions, government, education system and the corporate world have programmed into us our way of thinking and our core beliefs. We were programmed just as our parents were programmed, and likely how we will program our children. This is the nature of belonging and acceptance into our tribes. So long as we buy into any "group-think" (whether it serves our purpose or not), we will be accepted by them. This is a strength of the Material level of purpose.

Indeed, letting go of the programming on the Material level is probably the most difficult to attempt. There will be a lot of internal and external conflict in doing so. But it is the first step to living our purpose. Once we do it, we'll wonder why we waited so long to try.

As mentioned earlier, the ego is the place in which this programming resides. In fact, it is literally a construct created by the programming. As such, its primary purpose is to function as a constant reminder of our past; the past is the lens through which the ego views the current reality. It tells us what to think, what to say and what to do, based on how we've always done it and presumably how we will continue to do it. Rewind and play it again. It undermines our purpose. But it can only do that if we allow it to. We can prevent it from doing so using our awareness of what the ego really is.

On the Material level, the ego has a place. It gives us confidence and courage to compete with others, because that is its conditioned response as a matter of survival. But it also keeps us locked at this level. The ego has no awareness of anything beyond its programming, so whenever we try to create anything new, the ego chimes in about what it knows of us up to this moment. If we've always believed something about our self, the ego will remind us of this belief — be it that change is too hard, or we don't have the time, or we lack the money, or we're too sick, too weak, too this or too that. It will do so because all it knows at this point is *what we used to be like*. Thus, the ego is the very thing blocking our connection to the source of imagination because this connection can only be in the present and the ego is always oriented in the past.

Have you ever been so focused on what you are doing that it flows through you effortlessly? This is the release of our ego and connection to spirit-consciousness. It is turning off the old recording of the ego and playing something new.

There are only two states of mind we humans reside in. We are either "in spirit" or "in ego." When we are in ego, we can only react to situations as they present themselves in the same way we always did. When we are in spirit, we are able to create a new way of being. Being in spirit is a high energy creative state of mind, while ego is a low energy, preexisting state. Both states of mind cannot occupy our headspace at the same time, and so we bounce back and forth between the two, which is the reason we ride these waves of high and low energy as they manifest our reality. This mostly happens without our awareness, so we need to cultivate a mindset that creates this awareness.

Consider which state of mind you find yourself in throughout your day. Pay attention to how these states affect the way the day goes. This is how I clarify which state we are in: in Spirit, high energy thoughts become ideas, and ideas become the inspiration with which we take action by being proactive in creating our life. In Ego, low energy thoughts based on past experiences become emotional attachments to our past (i.e. how we've always reacted), and as situations arise, we can only emotionally react to them. We don't create our life when in ego. We only "react" to things outside us. Our reaction comes from our ego and how we react comes from how it was programmed.

The more mindful we are to our spirit state, the less we find ourselves being in the ego state. Pay attention to your state of mind and set your intention to reside in spirit. See how this plays out in your life. You can use the Three Elements of Purpose to help you here. In *everything* you do, ask yourself, *what* am I doing, *how* am I doing it, and *why* am I doing it? (It is the "why" of our purpose that we can clearly see whether or not our *intention* is derived from ego or spirit.) Then ask, "How does this serve my purpose?"

It is on the Material level of purpose that the ego has the most control over us. On the Ego level, the ego is more balanced with spirit, as we learn to lessen its influence over us. On the Altruistic level, the spirit has more control as we begin dissolving our ego until we reach the Enlightened level where the spirit has almost total control. We should, then, seek the Enlightened level of purpose. This can be a lifelong journey of silencing the ego and allowing the spirit to be the source of our energy.

Another way of identifying whether we are in an ego state of mind or in spirit is our emotions. Our emotions are our "state of mind" gauge or monitor. Low energy emotions of the ego include the anger, fear, worry, anxiety, et cetera that we developed through our past experiences and recorded in the ego, while the high energy emotions of being in spirit are peace, calm, happiness, contentment, et cetera that are more free-flowing in the present moment of connection. Think of our emotions as road signs we follow along our journey. Who wouldn't want to take the first exit to happiness? As we drive along, would any of us willingly take the exit marked sadness or anxiety? Yet somehow, we find ourselves on those negative paths. If our ego, via its programming, has been in low energy, it will always take the low road.

Try this experiment: as you go through your day, with everything you think, say or do, and with everyone and every situation you encounter, try taking your emotion out of it. Don't react immediately to anything or anyone. If someone says or does something that irritates or angers you (i.e. cuts you off in traffic) or makes you worried, anxious or fearful, just pause and be consciously aware of your emotion in the moment. See if you can get through one entire day without your emotions causing a reaction from you and see how you feel at the end of the day. This is not easy, given the strength of our programming and our ego, but it is possible and with practice, it gets easier.

This doesn't mean we should go through life emotionless, but rather become aware of the huge role our emotions play in our daily life. We'll realize that we really do allow our emotions to control us far too often, and if they are more on the negative side, then we are living too much of our life in an ego state of mind, which is always reactionary.

Think of everything we go through, be it an illness, a financial difficulty, issues in our relationships, the stress of our job, or any conflict we wish we could resolve. How much energy have we wasted dwelling on the problem from the perspective of the ego? How does that serve us and our purpose? We already know that conflict is necessary to our growth. We need to shift our focus to being more in spirit where we have clarity and it simply flows. We must stop allowing our ego (that voice in our head) to direct our attention toward, and then dwell on, our problems, for we will never be able to resolve them this way.

However, when we're in the calm and still spirit state of mind, we can allow our problems to just be what they are: necessary conflict. While in spirit it will become clear what action needs to be taken to resolve them. Solutions are simply opportunities hidden in problems. But we will not see problems in this manner so long as we allow our ego and its negative emotions to rule us.

If we want to change, then we must redefine ourselves. If we identify ourselves as spirits with a body, then the ego no longer holds power over us. Then and only then can we begin the real work of creating the life we truly want and fulfill our purpose.

Change isn't about changing the world to suit us, but rather changing ourselves to allow the world to just be what it is. Letting go of our ego is the key because it is letting go of our past. Only then have we gained the freedom with which we can create a new life.

There is another way to think about the ego and how our thoughts have been programmed. If we can understand it, we can control it.

Chapter Thirteen

I NEVER THOUGHT ABOUT IT
THAT WAY

There is nothing more powerful than thought. *Thought is energy.* Thought creates *everything.* The book you hold in your hands, the words you are reading, and the meaning derived from them are nothing more than my thoughts manifested onto the page, which you have allowed into your mind to contemplate and possibly use to make new connections or shifts. It is all energy being shifted around, creating something new that did not exist before.

Our thoughts have created everything that exists for us. The life we are currently living is a collection of thoughts, an illusion created for and by us. The life we have in the future will be created by the thoughts we choose to hold now. In order to create the future we want, we must cultivate awareness of those thoughts.

How do we do this? I have found it helpful to think of our brains like a computer (they are actually very similar). If we understand how a computer functions, we will also clearly see how we use (or don't use) our thought.

Within our computer-brain resides the hardware and software required to *operate our life.* The processor processes information we receive from the outside world; the memory chips are the temporary storage area of our thought. Our ego is the hard drive where all of the data of our thoughts and experiences are recorded and permanently stored.

The Consciousness of the Universe (or God) is the operating system developer of our life. Our set of beliefs are the individual operating systems available to us; we determine which operating system we prefer to live with, just as some people prefer the operating system of Apple, while others believe in Windows, Android, et cetera. This operating system is the belief system under which all our programs are run. These programs are written by our software development team — our parents, family, friends and the other groups we belong to. We too are programmers, though we seldom use this skill on ourselves. We don't think much of how we program our own mind.

Our first programmer was The Consciousness of the Universe (or God), and upon our conception our operating system was coded into us via our DNA, our genetics. As we developed into a baby, we had more hardware installed so we could sense our world to provide the data that got written to our hard drive. We were beginning to experience life, and so the programming had begun. After we were born and as we grew up our hardware was continually upgraded, and our software underwent continual revisions even as new software was installed.

Our parents were the most influential programmers of our software. They wrote the programs of our thoughts and beliefs that were run daily. Every morning we awoke and started up these programs, which then ran our life. Our purrents were the firewall, our protectors, who, per their own programming, allowed only so much of the outside world in to affect us. But as we grew older, our parents invited more of the outside world into our operating system, thus allowing more software developers into our life. They wrote new code into our mind, either by making revisions to existing software or installing new programs that allowed us to grow. In our youth we had very little control over what was installed. As adults we get to choose the software we want to run, yet few make any choice beyond those default programs.

Every day we awaken and start up our default programs. Sometimes these programs run efficiently and sometimes they develop glitches and do not operate the way we wish them to. This is the conflict in our life. Sometimes this is the case of a virus (negative thoughts) that needs antivirus software (positive thinking and affirmations); it can also be the fault of hardware that is failing (our health).

Now, we can take this conflict we face and resolve it by fixing or upgrading the hardware or software, thereby improving how our programs run. Each new and improved piece of hardware and software that resolves our conflicts is what we experience as growth. We can continue to limp along with faulty hardware, software and viruses, and simply put up with it (avoiding conflict, as most are prone to do), or we can make things right again, or even improve them. Far too many live with old, outdated computer hardware and software; they run the same programs day after day, year after year, then wonder why they remain stuck, unable to keep up with the inevitable changes in life.

The computer analogy is an excellent tool to help us understand the Theory of Purpose. Those who live in and remain stuck on the Material level of purpose are simply running old operating systems with outdated software that do not allow them to uplevel their thinking or their lives. If we are not using the power of our thought to create entirely new programs, we will continue to operate on the same level we always have.

If you want to really understand just how powerful our programming is, consider this: if our parents had raised us in isolation from the outside world, and from the moment of our birth and throughout our life they told us we were a chicken, we would identify ourselves as a chicken. If they told us to fear all humans, we'd be afraid of humans. If they said God was the Great Rooster King that would come and save us from humans, we'd believe God was a great Rooster, convinced we'd be saved by Him. Absurd as this idea is, we would in fact believe these things about ourselves and the world around us. It would be our truth. Still, something inside would gnaw at us, an internal knowing that something about being a chicken was wrong, but we wouldn't know why. Our ego would constantly try to convince us to remain the chicken it believes us to be and fight any attempt to discover that we are human. It doesn't know anything about being human because it was not programmed to know this.

As crazy as it sounds, this is exactly why we think and believe as we do, only instead of the Great Rooster King, we believe in Christ, Mohamed, Buddha, et cetera. Instead of believing we are chickens, we are convinced that we are these physical beings we call human, with all the limitations that go with that. We're programmed to grow up, get a job, put everyone else first, et cetera. Whatever we were programmed to think about ourselves and the world around us is exactly what we'll think and believe and not a bit of it was by choice. When we think about it, it's as absurd as being told to believe we're chickens!

The only answer is to become our own programmer, over-writing the old data and replacing it with new information with which to operate our life. But where do we come up with this new information or ideas with which to write this new software? Our imagination. Imagination is like a computer's network connection. Our spirit is connected to the Consciousness of the Universe (or God) much like a computer's data link to a network server, and if we allow it, the downloads we receive will be infinite. We can experiment with these new thoughts and choose only those that serve our purpose.

Remember that according to the Theory of Purpose *what we imagine we become* and that our *imagination is our only limitation*. Imagination is the playground of thought. So, we can use the power of thought and imagination to see possibilities in everything. Possibilities are created out of awareness, but in order to imagine without limits we need to have a bigger perspective and a greater awareness.

Chapter Fourteen

AN ASTRONOMICAL
PERSPECTIVE

If we are ever going to imagine with limitless possibilities, we first have to remove the limitation from our thoughts. I'm talking about a major shift in our thinking so that we understand not only our place within our family, society or even the global community, but our place in the entire Universe. I am talking about cultivating an *astronomical perspective*.

Most people seldom think about outer space; in fact, outside their favorite Science Fiction show they probably don't give it any contemplation at all. A relative few are aware that our planet is spinning like a top at nearly 1000 miles per hour. Just think about it — right now, at this very moment, we are traveling around the sun at a speed of around 67,000 miles per hour. Of course we can't feel ourselves moving and so, like so many things in life, this space flight is simply taken for granted.

We tend to think of our planet as the center of the Universe, a snow globe with pretty stars painted on the outer shell. Everything else is "out there." Even our closest celestial "neighbor," the Moon, is still almost a quarter-million miles away and only shows up at certain times throughout the month.

We take that for granted as well, despite the fact that it pulls all of our oceans along with it, and also affects our bodies. But again, why consider it when it doesn't seem to affect our daily life? We are too busy to notice or care.

All those pretty stars we see at night, if we notice them at all, are just like our Sun, yet some are so enormous they make it seem like the head of a pin. There are billions of them out there beyond our solar system, and yet some of those "stars" are entire galaxies far beyond our own Milky Way, containing billions of their own stars and planets. All of these stars and galaxies out in the Universe are dancing around each other at overwhelming distances and speed. Our solar system is racing around the core of the Milky Way at over *half a million miles per hour* and yet we cannot comprehend it. As fast as we are moving, it requires *one-quarter billion years* to circumnavigate it! And yet we are unaware, trapped in the ignorance of our own choosing.

Out of the billions of galaxies beyond our own, the closest is the Andromeda galaxy. We can actually see it with the unaided eye, though without a telescope we just see its bright core, mistaking it for a dim, fuzzy star. Andromeda is 2.5 million light years away and has a radius of 110,000 light years. A light year (the distance light travels in one earth year) is roughly six trillion miles, which means Andromeda is 2.5 million *times* six trillion miles away, and yet we can still see it because it is over *200,000 thousand light years* in diameter! Even with an expanded perspective it is difficult to grasp the enormity of scale and proportion of the Universe.

Here is something even more mind-blowing. If you've ever had the opportunity to see Andromeda through a telescope and under a dark sky, you know that you can see its spiral arms made of dust and billions of other stars of its own. As impressive a sight as it is, what's really amazing is that you are seeing what it looked like 2.5 million years ago, not how it is now. Why? Because that's how long it took for its light to reach our eyes. You are literally looking back in time! We won't see how it looks *now* for another 2.5 million years, not that we'll be alive to see it, of course. This is but one galaxy of such immense proportions and distance *out of billions.*

In 1995, the Hubble Space telescope took the world's most famous photo of our Universe. The astronomers pointed the Hubble at a region just above the Big Dipper that was *no larger than a pinhead held at arm's length*. The computer analysis of the photo revealed over 15,000 distinct galaxies in that singular speck of the sky, some of which were among the very first galaxies in existence when our Universe was first formed. Just take a moment to imagine this Universe *that we are currently aware of*. What kind of imagination is required to grasp the immensity of the Universe and our place in it?

Of all the things one can find out in the Universe, none are more relevant or symbolic to our purpose than nebulae. These giant clouds of gas are pure energy, condensing under the pressure of gravity to create new stars, bursting with the life force that created everything, including us.

Of the billions of nebulae, there is one that's easily visible to the naked eye: the Great Orion Nebula. Many have seen the winter constellation of Orion, the Hunter. Even the most novice of observers have seen the familiar "belt" of three bright stars, all in a neat straight line. What many do not realize is that just a bit below the left of these three bright stars lies two dim, fuzzy stars. The faintest of the two is not a star at all, but the Great Orion Nebula itself. It lies 1,344 light years (that's 1,344 times six trillion miles) away from Earth and yet we can see it because it is forty light years in diameter, or two-hundred-forty trillion miles wide. Four of the brightest stars (called the Trapezium) within the heart of this nebula are considered "very young," meaning they're only about a million years old.

The significance of this and other nebulae is not the enormity of them or their distance from us, but what they are and what they represent. Nebulae are often referred to as "stellar nurseries" or "star factories." To view a nebula is to witness the Consciousness of the Universe at work. One could then, from a different perspective, say they are seeing God at work (as if all of life isn't evidence enough). Even an atheist cannot deny the energy of the Universe is at work here, though they don't attribute it to the same source.

The same energy we see creating these stars lives within us. We are one with everything in the Universe. Understanding that this energy lives within us and gives us life is empowering. If this energy can take clouds of gas and turn them into stars, surely, we can do something less majestic and manipulate it into the life we desire. It is only in our limited thoughts and beliefs that we have no power to do so, despite the abundant evidence to the contrary that the Universe provides to us.

We don't need a telescope to see this evidence; in fact, one need look no further than our own Sun. It radiates this energy out into our solar system, giving and sustaining life on Earth. To see the Sun under the total solar eclipse is to glimpse this energy radiating out from it, shimmering out in the rays of its corona, out into a dark sky among other stars and planets in plain view, in the middle of the day. When one views the rare sight of totality from the perspective of oneness, it can be a life-transforming event, causing a major shift in how we see ourselves and the world around us in a profound way.

Imagine being Neil Armstrong, the first man to set foot on the Moon, as he looked back at the Earth and the rest of humanity. Imagine how such an experience would go right to the core of your being and alter your awareness of life. Edwin

Aldrin (the second man on the Moon) said upon his return that the experience changed his life forever. Edgar Mitchell, the astronaut aboard Apollo 14 and the sixth man to walk on the surface of the Moon, said that on his way back to Earth he had a powerful "savikalpa samādhi experience" (where the body is in a trance-like state but the consciousness is fully perceptive of its blissful experience within), which prompted him to create the Institute of Noetic Sciences for the purpose of consciousness research. These men didn't need to use their imagination, as their firsthand experience led directly to an incredible shift in their perspective. Yet we can use our imagination and wonder how it might change us as well.

If you're wondering what an eighth-grade science lesson has to do with personal growth or finding our purpose, consider this: due to our tribal programming, most people never move past the eighth-grade perspective. They continue to live life with this limited awareness and imagination, especially those dwelling on the Material level.

Of those who do increase their awareness, most still view everything from a limited earthbound perspective; they see Earth as the center of a random Universe and themselves as individuals struggling to get by. But if we can truly grasp our place in the Universe and understand the energy within us as the Consciousness of it, our perspective can shift dramatically towards our higher purpose in life.

Chapter Fifteen

THE SIGNIFICANCE IN THE INSIGNIFICANT

In the last chapter we attempted to shift our perspective by exploring the vastness of the Universe. Essentially, we discovered that we live on a very tiny ball of rock racing around a tiny star within a galaxy among billions of other stars with their own planets, among billions of other galaxies in the Universe. Makes us seem pretty insignificant, right? This leads me to another critical point, and another opportunity to shift our thinking. Just as we often fail to see the big picture, we also take the little things in life for granted, when in truth they can potentially bring great meaning to our life.

I want to share with you a story from my own life that led to a drastic shift in my perspective. In the 1990s I was a successful artist and I conducted art workshops to teach others about my tools and techniques. As successful as I was, at that point in my life and career I was going through the motions, running my default programs much as we all do.

On one ordinary morning, I was driving to a conference center for another workshop. This particular day was extremely windy, and as I drove along the trees captured my attention, with branches being blown about, twisting and bending to the will of the wind. Large groupings of trees were all swaying in concert with each other. I noticed how the color of their leaves changed as they moved about, revealing the lighter undersides one moment and the darker green of their tops the next. The trees were not just moving, they were shifting in patterns and color.

It was then that a flock of crows caught my eye. They too were being blown about by the wind. I thought how difficult it must be for them to fly in this weather, until I realized that they were not struggling, but playing in it! They swooped down in large arcs, then rose again as if on a rollercoaster made of air, performing aerobatics with all the skill of fighter pilots flying in tandem. My gaze shifted to the clouds beyond them, moving rapidly across the blue morning sky, shapeshifting in a myriad of colors reflecting the morning sun behind me. I realized I was looking at everyday things in an entirely new way. A new awareness was developed within me.

Why did I suddenly begin seeing these things this way? Certainly, I had seen trees, birds and clouds blowing in the wind before, as we all have. What was so significant about today that was different from any other windy day? *My awareness.* In this new awareness, I then mindfully looked at everything within my field of view this way. The grasses along the roadside were also dancing in the wind, with vast areas all around creating such interesting and ever-changing patterns. I noticed the gravel of the shoulder in such amazing detail, the pebbly pavement of the road and everything else within my senses were experienced in a deeper way. The ordinary things I always saw were now being experienced as extraordinary.

If I had never before seen all these things now being revealed to me with such clarity, what else had I been missing? I suddenly had an epiphany. The world around me didn't change. I did. I was filled with such excitement over the dis-covery of my awareness. Before that day, I might have been this observant of the birds or trees if they were the subject of a painting, but not in my physical reality. I began contemplating the meaning behind this. Moment by moment, day after day, I had been taking most everything in my life for granted; I was living in ego. But no longer.

I realized that the most important tool an artist has is a keen observation of the world around us. After that fateful drive, I not only became more observant, I found deeper meaning in everything I observed.

As with my other workshops, I had created a syllabus of sorts, outlining all the topics I would cover with my students. However, when I arrived at the conference center, I promptly threw my entire plan into the trash. I was no longer interested in teaching other artists how to draw or paint, but rather to be more observant and fully invested in life.

I'd always opened my workshops with the stock, rehearsed lecture, but today I was winging it without the crutch of my notes. I relayed to the class what I had discovered on my trip to the conference center, adding how I'd also received perhaps dozens of ideas for paintings. As I went around the room asking what the other artists noticed on their own drive there, I got the confirmation I was seeking. Most every artist in attendance was too preoccupied with the task of getting there to notice much of anything. They simply lacked awareness of the world around them, just as I had lacked it until my attention was grabbed by those dancing trees and frolicking crows.

Those few moments of my life serve as an example of what most of us do for much of our lives: we look at everything with a superficial glance, taking it for granted because we are too busy. We're so busy searching for that one big thing that will change our life that we pass by the little things that change our life moment by moment. Sometimes the very thing we're looking for — our purpose — is staring us right in the face, and we miss it due to this lack of awareness. Becoming observant and refining this skill can create that awareness and completely change our life.

We are all searching for meaning in our life. What we don't realize, however, is that the key to discovering our purpose and fulfilling it is found in the little things, because that is where purpose lies.

We can all find meaning and perspective in gorgeous sunsets, vast mountain ranges, the birth of a child or the death of a loved one. But how often are we going to experience the birth of a child? And sunsets are wonderful, but how many could we consider life-changing? If you are waiting on these relatively isolated moments to find meaning, you may have a very long wait indeed. However, if you will just open your eyes, you will see that all around us is beauty (recall the examples of the rain that ruined our plans and the "ugly" weed in our garden) in which you can find meaning. It's all a matter of perspective, and once we shift our mindset these "ordinary" things will reveal themselves to be anything but.

While we may not have the time to look at everything this way, we can train ourselves to be more consciously aware, allowing us to experience life through new, more observant eyes. The more we practice this, the easier it becomes, until one day we find ourselves doing it out of habit, consistently reminding ourselves how everything has its own significance and beauty, and how we are connected with it. This is what opens us and makes us more aware as human beings. If we are to get the most out of our purpose and derive meaning, we must search for meaning in *everything*. Take nothing for granted and be grateful for it all, from that vast mountain range to the dew drop on a single blade of grass.

This is the fabric of life, the Consciousness of the Universe manifested in its creation of all that is, including us. We are all connected. That makes us pretty significant.

Significance in the insignificant is a paradox, as all of life truly is.

Chapter Sixteen

THE DUALITY OF LIFE

Under heaven all can see beauty as beauty,

only because there is ugliness.

All can know good as good only because there is evil.

Being and non-being produce each other.

The difficult is born in the easy.

Long is defined by short, the high by the low.

Before and after go along with each other.

So the sage lives openly with apparent duality

and paradoxical unity.

The sage can act without effort and teach without words.

Nurturing things without possessing them,

he works, but not for rewards;

he competes, but not for results.

When the work is done, it is forgotten.

That is why it lasts forever.

~Lao Tzu, The Tao Te Ching

*I*n this chapter, let's suspend our notion of reality and play with our imagination for a bit. Remove all limitations and just imagine how things might be different for us. Imagine an alternate reality.

Ever since the release of the 2004 movie, *What the Bleep Do We Know!?,* more and more people have become aware of and fascinated with quantum physics and its application in our everyday lives. Scientists, however, have been exploring this world for over a century, some with the particular focus on the theory that the past, present and future are all happening simultaneously (though this theory did not originate with the study of quantum physics and actually has been considered for millennia). Einstein himself said, *"People like us, who believe in physics, know that the distinction between past, present and future is only a stubbornly persistent illusion."*

The idea that as you read this in your "present" moment, you both have yet to be born *and* have already died, is something our conscious mind has a difficult time grasping. It is in complete conflict with our programming, which is based on linear time.

I have found Taoist philosophy particularly useful in helping me understand the idea of our past, present and future existing simultaneously. Nothing so simply exemplifies this philosophy as the second verse of the *Tao Te Ching* (cited at the very beginning of this chapter), specifically the fourth line, *"Being and non-being produce each other."* But what does this mean?

Taoism is both a religion and a philosophy, based on the idea of Yin/Yang. In ancient Chinese philosophy, yin and yang is a concept of dualism, i.e. — how seemingly opposing or competing forces may not only be complementary, inter-connected, and cooperative in the natural world, but may actually *produce* each other. Taoism is basically about balance and harmony; thus it is a philosophy that allows one to easily achieve peace and contentment. The line *"Being and non-being produce each other,"* shows us that both "being" and "non-being" must exist simultaneously for there to be balance. They are one and the same, and only our perspective has us *experiencing* one or the other in any given moment.

Taoism is circular in thought, with no beginning and no ending. No physical evidence is required of either, as it is a given that they *both exist/don't exist simultaneously*, or neither can exist. It is within this philosophy of Yin/Yang that we can easily resolve the idea of our past/present/future as being one singular thing. We know that the past cannot exist without there also being a future, and it is in our "present" moment that we experience our perspective and achieve balance and harmony with all. This philosophy extends to all things in life, be it happiness/sadness, life/death, contentment/discontentment, love/hate, success/failure, et cetera. Understanding the Taoist "way" is a key to a happy life, and how we can attract the life we desire, if only we can get out of our *own* way.

By contrast, Western thought is very linear, distinct and rigid, requiring physical evidence of existence. Instead of the concept of duality central to Taoist thinking, Western philosophy holds that everything is in opposition, *competing* for our attention and desire. There is neither balance nor harmony because everything is "either/or" and therefore causes tension and struggle rather than peace and contentment. This linear thinking, coupled with the requirement of physical evidence, is what makes our programming so easy to accept — *"There is the evidence, so it must be true."*

In Western thought, there is a logical progression to life whereby the programming gets reinforced at every step along this linear path. We are born and raised by our parents, accepting of the beliefs passed onto us because the evidence suggests it must be true. We go onto school and accept the programming of our educational institutions. We then go out into society, get jobs to support ourselves and accept the programming of the workforce and society. We get married, have children, work until retirement and then possibly enjoy our end years (if healthy enough to do so) and then we die. We see most everyone around us living this way, thus providing us with the physical evidence we need to accept it as truth.

While on the surface this viewpoint may make life seem simpler (in the sense that we can operate on autopilot), it actually makes it much more difficult. We do not seek balance. We seek happiness, and we will not be happy until there is evidence of it, usually in the form of material things (i.e. a home, a new car, a career, a diploma or degree, a husband, wife, children, and so on). In the acquisition of this thing or things, we briefly feel happiness, only to find the feeling wears off as quickly as the appeal of the thing itself. We are then off seeking another thing to replace it and thus recapture that feeling of happiness. This is the Material level of purpose.

The Eastern, Taoist view of life is entirely different. Being circular and accepting of the duality of life, we do not seek happiness. Instead, we seek balance, which brings contentment. It is in contentment that happiness is found. We then no longer need to continually search for this elusive thing we call happiness. It just exists, because it was always there, right along with our unhappiness. They both must exist, or neither exists. What we believe we attract, so if we believe we are unhappy (until the evidence suggests otherwise), we may be unhappy for a very long time. Just as the continual search for it exists, so does the struggle and discontent.

In the Taoist, circular, view there is no need to follow a rigid timeline of life. In duality, time is not linear and therefore this opens possibilities and we are offered freedom. The thinking of

Taoist duality is difficult to program because it requires no evidence, and there is no stationary marker telling us where we need to be at any point in life. Because in Taoism we seek balance, we no longer need to chase after those "things" we've been programmed to believe we must acquire in order to be happy. In a dualistic view, materialism is also simultaneously immaterial.   Dualism suggests a paradox whereby something cannot *exist* without it also *not existing.* To understand this Taoist concept, let's look at the notion of happiness.

Suppose we spent our entire life, from the moment of our birth to when we take our last breath, being totally happy, not once experiencing sadness. For us, happiness would then not exist. Why is this? Because if our entire life was filled only with happiness, *we wouldn't know what it was,* as there would be nothing to compare it to in order to define it. Without the awareness and knowledge of sadness, happiness would be unknown to us. How could we ever *be* happy, if we don't *know* what being happy is?

So it is with *everything* in life.

In Taoism all things exist in a paradoxical harmony, allowing us to gain perspective of our world. Nothing exists for us *in our current reality* without our awareness of its existence. Whatever thought or belief we hold is held simply out of our awareness of it. We cannot possibly know of any other way to think because another way to think simply *doesn't exist* in our mind. This is why it can be so difficult to change the way we think or believe. Our Western programming told us that "this is what *exists,*" so when we run into a thought or belief counter to what exists in our mind, we suffer from internal conflict. In Taoism, this conflict is easily resolved because we are already aware that with any thought, its counterpart must exist.

What does this duality have to do with our purpose? Remember that our purpose is our *reason for being.* Awareness comes into play here. We seek things because we cannot find them. We are mindful only of that which we are experiencing in our current reality. In duality, existence/non-existence are the same. It is only our perspective from our present reality that creates our awareness, so it isn't that these things we seek do not exist. They are simply not within our awareness, so in this illusion they only *appear* to not exist. We seek our purpose because we are aware of having *no purpose*. We seek happiness because we are aware of *not being happy*. We seek wealth because we are aware of *not being wealthy*. We seek peace because we are aware of *not being at peace*. We seek health because we are aware of *not being healthy*. We've been programmed to *believe only in the evidence of our current reality*. This is what holds us back from what we desire.

It is the faulty programming of "We will believe it when we see it," that leaves us placing our attention on that which is currently in our awareness, or the very things we *believe* are real. And we will dwell obsessively on what we don't want, or what we are not being because that is our current reality. We *believe* it is so, and so it is. Per Western thought, the evidence proves us right.

Here is where our *intention* comes into play. If happiness is our intention, putting our attention on unhappiness will leave us unaware of happiness and so the illusion is that happiness does not exist for us. We can't imagine being happy because the belief is in our unhappiness. The evidence supports the belief.

What we need to do is stop dwelling on *that which we don't want,* or what we are currently experiencing as undesirable. When we stop dwelling on (or believing in) our problems, the solutions will appear. When we are suffering, we need to stop dwelling on that which causes us to suffer, and relief will reveal itself. If we want to discover our purpose, then we must stop believing we lack purpose.

God will never reveal to us anything we are not ready for. We cannot be ready to attract something we don't believe in. The Theory of Purpose states that *"What we believe we attract and what we imagine we become."* Our imagination is only limited by our beliefs.

By understanding duality, we can apply the Theory of Purpose, knowing our purpose exists, believing in it, imagining ourselves living it, and then via our thoughts create the circumstances with which to manifest it.

This is living with purpose. Imagine that.

Chapter Seventeen

LIVING ON PURPOSE

It is no accident that we were born. I'm not talking about whether our parents planned on having us. I'm talking about our spirit needing to be born into a physical body in order to experience life through it. The Theory of Purpose states, *"We are the manifestation of the Consciousness of the Universe, co-creating and manifesting our life into existence."* Thus, the Consciousness of the Universe (God) experiences life through us as well. There is purpose for life. *All life.* We may choose to believe, depending on our programming, in randomness or things happening accidentally, but the truth is that everything in the Universe happens on purpose and for a specific reason. Upon our birth, we were given both a specific purpose to fulfill and this universal purpose of manifesting God in all that we do.

Once we fully understand that our life is no accident, we will realize that we should not be living it by accident. Yet this is exactly what we do, especially on the lower levels of purpose. We have been programmed to be reactionary with almost everything. We spill our coffee or burn the toast "by accident" and then react to it, when in reality if we were living on purpose, we would be mindful of the bread in the toaster or where and how we placed our cup of coffee. But when we live accidentally, we set no intention to be careful and then pay no attention to that intention, and — voila! — accidents happen.

Living on purpose means that in all that we do, with both the grand and mundane, we set an intention, we act on that intention, and then we pay attention to it. This is mindfulness, and through it we remove the accident from the equation. If we live our life on purpose in all that we do, we take randomness out of the equation as well, which gives us an immense amount of power and control over our life.

Living *on* purpose is about taking that control and directing it towards fulfilling our purpose. Thus, fulfilling our purpose and living *on purpose* are interchangeable.

When we are not living with purpose, life can feel like a game of dodgeball, with us darting this way and that to avoid getting hit in the gut. When we take control of our life, we no longer react to people or situations out of our emotional state (our ego state of mind) but rather in our spiritual awareness, we set our intentions and then mindfully take action. We are then no longer blindsided by life, but are always prepared and act accordingly, without emotion sabotaging our efforts. We see what things life is throwing our way, long before they arrive.

When we live on purpose, we know we will become what we imagine. Living on purpose means we do not require evidence in our current reality to believe in the future we wish to create. Living on purpose is a willingness to change our current thoughts and beliefs.

When we can say, "I know my beliefs to be true *because I know they must change,*" then we are making some progress because we are open to accepting new truths. Yes, this will cause conflict for us to resolve, which is also good news, for it's an opportunity to stop living from our old programs and begin living on purpose. We begin to shed previous limitations and set new intentions where all things become possible. Recall that the

Theory of Purpose states that *"as a manifestation of the Consciousness of the Universe we also evolve and co-create with the Universe."* As co-creators of the Universe, we have no limitations. We can literally attract everything we need to create the life we desire.

Chapter Eighteen

THE LAW OF ATTRACTION

It should be obvious that the more positive thoughts we have, the more positive people and situations we attract into our life. Conversely, the more negative thoughts we have, the more negative we become, and so, as the saying goes, "misery loves company," we invite more like-minded people into our negative world. That said, being a ray of sunshine, positive and happy, does not mean that we attract *only* that into our life. We simply increase the likelihood. We will still sometimes attract negative people and situations; just know that we attracted them as a source of conflict, a dualistic opportunity to grow. Attraction is like a magnet, drawing some things to us while simultaneously repelling others, depending whether they are positively or negatively charged.

For good or for bad, this is how we have created our life. Where you are in life right now is entirely due to your past thoughts, beliefs and what you imagined yourself to be (from whatever circumstances you were in). We might have been born with some physical limitation, or others have imposed their limitations onto us, or perhaps we have experienced great trauma or lived in less than ideal circumstances. All of this, no matter how painful or challenging, is nothing but our current reality from which to grow. What we do with what we've been given is entirely up to us.

The Law of Attraction states that "like attracts like" and that in order to attract what we wish we must resonate at the vibrational frequency of this desire. But what does this really mean and how can we come to understand it?

The perfect analogy to describe the Law of Attraction, and how we can resonate at the vibrational frequency of what we desire, is music. Music is mathematical and, as Italian astronomer and physicist Galileo Galilei said, "Mathematics is the language in which God has written the Universe."

Everything in the Universe resonates at a particular frequency, including us. Being a performing musician most of my life, I understand resonant frequencies and creating music with others all too well. We can equate the Law of Attraction to music by understanding frequencies and how they must resonate together in order to produce (manifest) beautiful music.

Every note on the musical scale has a frequency, which is measured in hertz. Let's take the "A" note. Modern standard tuning is based on the frequency of 440 Hz. The musical note "A" resonates at 440Hz when tuned properly. The octaves of "A" resonate at perfect intervals of 440 Hz, so every octave of the "A" note on the scale will perfectly resonate as 55Hz, 110Hz, 220Hz, 440Hz, 880Hz and so on.

Recall from the chapter on duality that "Being and non-being produce each other" (therefore "like and unlike produce each other), and the Taoist philosophy of Yin/Yang, which holds that the ideal is being *in harmony* and *balance* with the Universe. Beautiful music is produced when it is harmonious.

Let's use a guitar for this musical example. The strings of a guitar, when plucked, vibrate, producing sound. Each string, (and every note on it) resonates at its own frequency. In order for our musical instrument to resonate in perfect harmony with itself, it must be tuned properly. As mentioned above, "A" resonates at 440Hz, therefore the open "A" string on the guitar must be tuned precisely to that frequency. All other strings must then be tuned to this scale, each at their own resonant frequency. It is only when the guitar's strings are perfectly tuned to each other that it will produce beautiful music when played. Applying this concept to the Law of Attraction, we are the instrument and we must ensure that we are tuned to the right vibrational frequency.

Taking this musical analogy further, if we wish to produce (manifest) music with other musicians, we can only co-create with them and produce a beautiful harmonious sound by matching our frequency with theirs. In other words, not only must we ensure that our instrument is in tune with itself, it must also be in tune with whomever we co-create music with. It is only when our instruments are in tune together that it is possible to produce the beautiful music we desire. If we are even the slightest bit off, with our instrument being either sharp or flat, out of tune with itself and the other musicians, we cannot resonate together in perfect harmony.

If we think of the Consciousness of the Universe as the co-creator of this music we wish to create, we must match the vibration of Its resonant frequency or the result will be an audible mess of sound. Our life is exactly like this. When we are not in tune with our self, and are not resonating with a matching frequency of our co-creator, our life will be a mess and we will cringe at the reality produced, much like we do when listening to musicians who are not in harmony with one another.

When it comes to the Law of Attraction, whatever we wish to attract we must be in harmony with, or match the frequency of, *perfectly*. If we are off, even slightly, we will not attract what we desire. According to the Taoist philosophy of Yin/Yang ("like and unlike produce each other"), when we are not in tune with the vibrational frequency of our desire, we will in fact produce "unlike" (or what we do NOT wish to attract). We might then think the Law of Attraction does not work or that like does not attract like. The reality is we are simply not in tune with our self, nor are we in tune with our co-creator, the Consciousness of the Universe (God). Now the question becomes, how do we "tune" our life to vibrate with the Consciousness of the Universe?

Let's go back to the beginning of the book where we explored the elements of purpose. Think of the Three Elements of Mind and the Three Elements of Purpose as the six strings of our guitar in the music analogy above, except that here all must be tuned so that they're vibrating with the frequency of our desire in any one of the Six Elements of Life (Career, Finances, Health, Relationships, Spirituality or Personal Growth).

For example, in order to attract good health, all six elements must be in tune. We will start with the Three Elements of Mind, which are our thought, beliefs and imagination.

Thought. *What we think, we create.* In order to create good health, we must have the thought of it. Typically we only think of creating it when we are *ill.* It is in the dualistic idea of health/illness (where "health and illness produce each other") that our thoughts about it are seldom very clear. Our perspective will only reveal one or the other, even while (according to Taoist circular thought) both exist simultaneously. In Western linear thought, we rely so much on the evidence of our current reality that our thoughts can be very blurred between health and illness. When we are ill, our thoughts dwell on illness because this is what the evidence shows us. Remember, however, that *What we think, we create.* When our thought is about illness, this is what we continue to create. To become in tune with the desire of attracting good health, we must think only of good health and disregard the evidence of illness.

Once our thought is in tune with "good health," we then turn our attention to the second element of the mind, *beliefs*. We can never attract that which we do not truly believe in, for "*What we believe, we attract.*" In this case, what we wish to attract is good health. To be in tune with and "vibrate" it, we must once again disregard the current evidence of being ill and *believe ourselves to already be* in good health. The depth of our belief will determine what we attract. Any doubt whatsoever keeps us out of tune with good health and therefore prevents it from showing up in our physical reality.

With our thought and belief in tune with good health, we now use the third element of the mind, *imagination*, and *visualize* ourselves already being in good health. In our imagination we clearly see ourselves being healthy and thus become so because "*What we imagine, we become.*"

Now that our Three Elements of the Mind are in tune with each other, we can begin to consciously work with the Law of Attraction because we are creating, believing in and imagining our good health. However, in order to vibrate with and attract good health, we must tune up three more elements, namely the Three Elements of Purpose (intention, expression and manifestation).

Like our thought, our *intention* must be very clear, leaving no doubt as to what we wish to attract. We cannot set our intention on "not being ill," as this intention is still focused on illness and thus will continue to attract illness. Our intention must be solely on good health. It is with our intention that the second element of purpose, *expression*, is enacted.

Once our intention is perfectly tuned in and vibrating harmoniously with good health, we then express this intention via mindfulness (which is simply "paying attention to our intention"). Our expression of good health is in doing the things necessary to attract good health. We will eat nutritious, healthy foods and we will either rest or exercise as needed to optimize our body to receive good health.

Expression is the element of purpose that goes out of tune the most. We can focus our thought and intention on good health, and we can believe and imagine we will be healthy, but if we behave in a way that is out of alignment with this desire (i.e. eating poorly) it will not manifest.

This is a common misconception about the Law of Attraction — that we do not need to take any action; that we can simply set our intention then let it go and allow it to happen. The truth is, for "like to attract like," the *expression* of our desire must also vibrationally match it. The actions that attracted illness in the first place must be "retuned" in order for us to vibrate with the desire for good health.

The last element we must tune is the third element of purpose, *manifestation*. Manifestation *is the vibration* with which we attract our desire. This element of purpose is what the Law of Attraction means by stating that we must be vibrating with the frequency of our desire. Manifestation is our vibration, or what we are sending out into the Universe.

When any of the Six Elements of Purpose are not in tune with each other, we are in a vibrational mismatch and though *like attracts like*, this mismatch (or being out of tune) will *appear* to attract unlike. As duality states, "like and unlike produce each other," so when we are not in tune, we attract not what is desired but a lesson to be learned, or as mentioned in the chapter on the Two Elements of Meaning, *conflict*. According to the Theory of Purpose, it is in the resolution of conflict that we learn, grow and derive meaning. This then allows us to get back in tune with what we *do* wish to attract. If we are aware, we will understand that conflict gives us the opportunity to gain clarity of purpose and our true intentions.

The Consciousness of the Universe (God) is *always* in tune.

When all of our six elements (*thought, belief, imagination, intention, expression, manifestation*) are in tune with each other, we can vibrate and co-create with God to harmoniously produce this beautiful music.

God is Love; thus, when we are in tune and vibrate with the resonant frequency of God we will then manifest the binding element of our universal purpose: Love. Out of this Love we will then express our purpose in the Six Elements of Life and create fulfilling careers, wealth, good health, loving and lasting relationships (with our self and others), spiritual enlightenment and personal growth. The more mindfully we manifest Love, the higher levels of purpose we can attain. This is how the Law of Attraction works.

Chapter Nineteen

THE COMPANY WE KEEP

We all seek a connection with others. We need it in order to express Love. The relationships we establish are extremely important to our well-being, and none more so than the relationship we have with our own self. We are taught to put others first, and as noble as that is, it often results in everyone getting shortchanged. When we keep giving away our time, energy and Love to others without investing in ourselves, eventually there will be little left of our self to give. This isn't to say that we should never put the needs of another above our own, but we must be aware of our own energy level when we are around others.

We've all felt the immediate and strong sensation of energy we humans vibrate with and emanate. Walk into any funeral and it can feel like a black hole, a deep void or vacuum of energy being sucked out, leaving all in very low energy. That is to be expected. On the other hand, when walking into a wedding or birthday celebration we can just feel the positive vibration of energy from everyone.

This energy exists always, in all of us. The positive and negative energy flow of life. But life isn't always weddings and funerals, and in most circumstances we will not sense such obvious energetic extremes. In fact, it is easy to go through much of our life recognizing no energy whatsoever. This is what most will do.

We all have this instinct or "gut feeling" about people and situations. This is a reaction to the energy level being put out there for us to feel. But we tend to not follow our feeling about this energy, and instead attempt to make logical decisions based on the ego's programming.

People can be very charming in their appearance, saying and doing all the seemingly right things that draw us to them. People can also put us off by their words and actions. These are the superficial qualities our logical ego mind perceives. But deep down, we will often have a feeling about others without logical thought. This ease or unease is either a vibrational match or disturbance to our field of energy. This does not mean that there is anything right or wrong with that person. It only means we feel comfortable or uncomfortable around them, in a given situation. Under a different set of circumstances you might not feel the same way about that person. Again, this isn't a judgment of him or her, but a reaction to their energy in the moment. We should be aware and mindful of this energy, for it will serve us well and often better than the logical mind.

The people we choose to surround ourselves with are mostly chosen for logical, ego-driven reasons. We have things in common with them, such as with our friends, or we feel obligation to be with them, as with our family members, or we must cooperate with them, as with coworkers. There are perfectly legitimate and even healthy reasons for allowing certain people into our lives, none of which has to do with their energy.

In fact, we seldom pay attention to the energy of the people around us. We will notice the obvious, such as those who make us feel very strong emotions, either good or bad. We will love being around those who make us smile or laugh or despise being around people who frustrate or anger us. Most, however, fall into the energetic soup we encounter every day and largely ignore, at least on a conscious level.

Whether we realize it or not, the energy of others affects us and, depending on our awareness or lack thereof, may even affect our perspective and life choices as well. In order to build conscious awareness of the energy of others, we must first become more in tune with our own energy. We are of little to no use in helping anyone, including ourselves, when we are in a low energy state of being. In those moments, we need to turn our attention inward and work on raising our own energy, not wasting what little we have on others. We often call this "recharging." Have you ever felt energetically depleted but kept on giving to others out of obligation or a need to be accepted? Have you then reacted from this depleted energy state, which manifested outwardly as frustration, anger, et cetera? If you had instead taken a step back and gave yourself a little time to "recharge," the result probably would have been very different.

Again, it all comes down to the relationship we have with ourselves. We need to learn how to love ourselves, just as we are. We need to learn how to raise and maintain our energy level through self-care in all the Six Elements of Life. When we love all aspects of ourselves, we cease being judgmental of others because we no longer need to seek validation in them. When we have high, positive energy within, we exude or emanate positive energy towards others and thus attract more people who do the same. They will be naturally drawn to us because we will be living our purpose.

This is when we most need to be aware of our energy, for in addition to the high-energy people we will also attract those living in lower energy. Some we can assist and guide towards higher energy. Others, however, are so needy that they must feed off the energy of others to recharge themselves because they cannot do so on their own. Some call these people "energy vampires," but I don't like to think of them in this manner. They are just lost souls, trying to find their own purpose but have no one to guide them in a positive way. These are people who think mostly negative thoughts, live with faulty beliefs and complain about life but make no attempt to change it. It's not because they won't. It is because they don't know how and so will remain stuck in low energy. Being aware of our own energy is invaluable here, if we are to truly live our purpose (expressing Love).

We can be of help to those who are lost, so long as we are living in the higher levels of purpose. It is difficult to help those in the Material Level if we too reside there. This is where the entire idea of "misery loves company" comes from. People living in low energy, who cannot raise their own energy, wish to be in the sympathetic company of others who also cannot raise their energy. Instead of being lifted to higher states of energy, they all wallow in the low energy together. They are simply unaware and nothing more. If we are living in a higher state of energy, we can aid them, but only if they are willing to make a commitment to change.

We can be one of those who live in low energy but wish to change. We may also have some aspects of our being that vibrate in low energy, even while other aspects are in high energy. This is the internal conflict we deal with. Those living in low energy are there because they avoid conflict rather than embracing it and resolving it. Growth, and raising our energy, requires conflict and resolution. Avoiding conflict always keeps us in low energy.

The energy we put out there is always going to draw people who are either emanating the *same energy*, or those who are in need of this *same energy*. When two or more people living in high energy are in each other's field of energy, their combined energy is raised. When two or more people living in low energy are in each other's field of energy, their combined energy is lowered. When one in high energy is in the field of one in low energy, the high energy is lowered and the low energy is lifted to create balance. Energy always lives in balance. It's the natural harmony of the Universe. This is important to be aware of when it comes to the company we keep.

Those who work in the helping professions (nurses, doctors, police officers, EMTs, therapists, coaches, et cetera) are constantly subjected to people who are in lower energy states. Aside from their colleagues, they almost never see people at their best, and often see them at their worst. When we are continually immersed in low energy, self-care is not a recommendation but a necessity. In fact, lack of self-care is the reason so many in the helping professions burn out or suffer from PTSD and depression.

No matter what we do for a living, we all need self-care — physically, mentally and energetically. If we become aware of our own energy, we will begin to notice the energy of others and protect ourselves from those living in a lower energetic state.

Look at the company we keep – be it our family, friends, coworkers and everyone we come into contact with. How is our energy when we are around them? If we are aware and mindful, we will begin seeing who in our life facilitates our expression of our purpose and who holds us back from expressing it.

So you see, personal growth is really energy work. When we are living in purpose, and expressing it out of Love, we are emanating the highest levels of energy. On the Material level of purpose, we hold tightly onto our energy, and thus remain trapped in our false beliefs that this is just how life is. Those on the Enlightened level of purpose no longer hold energy, for they realize we are but a conduit for the energy of the Universe and allow it to flow through them in an endless supply of Love. This is our universal purpose, and the level we need to seek.

Chapter Twenty

COMMITMENT

"The journey of a thousand miles begins with the first step."

~ Lao Tsu

The gist of the very famous quote above is that even the most overwhelming task can be tackled if we have the strength and the will to begin. While I deeply revere this great Chinese philosopher and founder of Taoism, I take a slightly different view of the thousand-mile journey. I contend that the most difficult part of changing one's life is not taking that first step; it's not giving up before we take the last one. This requires commitment.

Let's say, for example, that reading this book is the first step in your journey. While everything discussed so far is important to consider, they are in fact only concepts and embracing them conceptually is not going to change your life much. Of course, thinking in a more spiritually and/or positive way will benefit you. How can it not? The more effort we put into thinking positively, the more positive life becomes. However, in order to create the life you desire, you will not only have to understand these concepts but begin applying them to your thoughts, beliefs, intentions and actions. Lasting change comes from daily, ritualistic habits that become routines. These routines become our new lifestyle. This takes a lot of work, and a lot of time. It took our entire life to get where we are right now, and it's going to take a serious commitment to shifting those underlying thoughts and beliefs, resolve conflict, and create something new.

No matter how much effort we put into creating our life, we will inevitably experience some failures along the way. But the failures don't mean it's not working; in fact, they are gifts and opportunities to see what we are doing wrong so we can then adjust and make corrections to our way of thinking or acting. In this way, failures can be viewed as internal conflict. We can learn and grow by resolving them, *eventually* turning them into success. This is where commitment comes into play.

Success, on the other hand, can actually cause us to *stop* growing. Before you slam the book shut, just hear me out. I am not knocking success. Success is wonderful! That said, it simply does not provide the types of opportunities for growth that failure does. What do I mean by this? We often set goals and do what we need to in order to achieve them, only to then fall back into old habits again because we have not done the underlying spiritual work needed to create sustainable change. The most common example is weight loss. We set a goal to lose a certain number of pounds or inches, or to reach a certain weight. We choose from the plethora of nutritional and exercise plans out there, and over time we meet our goal. Success! But what typically happens? Life moves on, we eventually stop thinking so much about our diet and exercise regimen, and the number on the scale begins to creep back up. This is because we were focused on that one thing — the goal weight — rather than the process of expressing Love to ourselves through a healthy lifestyle.

Do you see now how success can trip us up? In order to truly create what we want, we need to change *how we think* about change itself. We aren't trying to change ourselves *until we reach a goal.* We are trying to permanently change the way we live *for the rest of our life.*

Commitment is the promise we make to not give up on ourselves. When we make commitments to others, they let us know when we have not fulfilled them. They hold us accountable. Promises to ourselves are much easier to break. It's like cheating at Solitaire — only we will know. Promises to ourselves are also easier to justify breaking. We have been programmed to think it's much worse to cheat others than it is to cheat ourselves. Again, it all stems from a lack of self-love. Once we make the decision to love ourselves no matter what, sustainable change will come easier to us. We will hold ourselves accountable.

Another reason we lack commitment is that we often take our own lives for granted, thinking we always have tomorrow or the rest of our lives to do this personal growth work. This is procrastination, pure and simple. As someone once said, "It isn't that you can't. It's that you won't." If we are unhappy with any aspect of our life, isn't the very reason for our unhappiness that we've spent our entire life putting it off? If we don't make the commitment now, when will we?

Personal growth takes time alone, yet we seldom take this time for ourselves. We have been programmed to consider this "selfish," and because we've all learned that to be selfish is bad, we tell ourselves we will do this sacred work after we've fulfilled our obligations to others. On the rare occasion we do think of ourselves first, we find that others are disappointed or angry. They try to make us feel guilty and, depending upon what level of purpose we're on, we accept that guilt and put our own needs back on the shelf to be revisited later. In the meantime, our precious life is slipping away, day by day and moment by moment.

Commitment to personal growth is necessary to our purpose. Are we really giving all that we can to others when we aren't at our best? As mentioned earlier, when we don't take the time to be our best we are not only shortchanging ourselves but those we care about. We deserve better than that, and so do they.

We need to look at ourselves as the most important person in our life. We should, as mentioned in the evaluation section, put ourselves at the top of the list of those we love. When we create the life we want, we become happier, more content, and fulfilled. When we see that our life has purpose, our life improves, as do the lives of those around us. It's a win-win. But it takes a shift in our perspective as to how we see ourselves, how much we love ourselves and how willing and committed we are to being selfish; how much we dare to be great.

Chapter Twenty-One

OUR PHYSICAL WELL-BEING

The single biggest detriment to our well-being is stress and how we deal with it. My good friend Bill Cortright, a top-selling author and an expert on wellness, has done some excellent work around stress mastery. Using the science of the mind-body connection, Bill has created practical methods to deal with stress and I highly encourage you to check out his teachings. In the meantime, I turn to the role stress plays in undermining our purpose.

There was a time when humans were truly under stress, as in imminent physical danger, on a regular basis. If we were being stalked by a saber-toothed tiger, our body filled with adrenalin and other stress hormones that prepared us to either battle the tiger or try to escape. This is called the "fight or flight response," and it triggers a host of physiological changes that place a heavy burden on the body. However, assuming we survived and were safe again, the body returned to its normal, healthy state. This is part of our physical makeup that we still carry with us today, and herein lies the problem.

For the most part, we rarely face such imminent physical risks today. However, we have different kinds of stress, and far more of it, in our modern society, not the least of which is the stress we impose upon ourselves. Our bodies cannot differentiate between stressors. Things like being late to work, traffic jams or people cutting us off in traffic, and countless other things all cause our bodies to react in the exact same way as an attack from a saber-toothed tiger. If our body remains in this stressful state, our health will eventually deteriorate.

It stands to reason then that the best way to deal with this stress is to maintain a physically healthy body through diet and exercise.

Remember that on the Material level we take our health for granted. We assume that health is a given and illness is just a random act of bad luck, so we take no personal responsibility for either. On the lower levels of purpose, diet and exercise are for the most part superficial attempts.

I'm neither a physical fitness trainer nor a dietitian so I will not go into specific plans or goals to work on in this book. There are a wide variety of people who specialize in these areas and I urge you to find someone to help you create a regimen that works for you. What I do know is that we need to be physically active in some way. It doesn't matter if it is walking, running, jogging, yoga, aerobics, weightlifting, et cetera — we need to keep moving in any way we can, no matter what state our bodies are currently in. Nothing will erode our physical health faster than sitting or lying around most of the day and night.

Rest is another requirement for physical and mental health, so it is critical that we get an adequate amount of quality sleep. Staying up late and working long hours might accomplish more in some areas of life, but if it is sabotaging our physical or mental health in the process, we are most definitely not living with purpose.

As mentioned earlier in the book, what we eat plays an enormous role in our physical health. I am not talking here about "going on a diet" to lose weight, but a complete change in how we think about food and what we consume so that healthy eating becomes habitual. There is no cheating and no shortcuts, which means no cookie cutter fad diets. It has to be a lasting change that you'll love making part of your new lifestyle.

The next time you're faced with the temptation to eat some delicious but unhealthy food, ask yourself if you love eating it more than you love being healthy. The answer is obvious. Remember, purpose is a process, and when we love ourselves and express that Love by eating properly and exercising, we are demonstrating commitment to that process. We are also improving our physical health and thus building a strong foundation from which to care for our mental health.

Chapter Twenty-Two

FOOD FOR THOUGHT

The molecular structure of a sponge is such that it will soak up any fluid it comes in contact with. It has no mechanism to detect a benign liquid from a poisonous one; nor does it have a filter to prevent one type of fluid from being absorbed. Our brains are similarly structured in the way that they absorb information. We are literally bombarded with millions of bits of information each day via our five senses. Everything in our environment, either directly or indirectly, becomes a part of our reality. Like the sponge, all of what our subconscious mind soaks up and retains is placed in there without our consent or even awareness, and some of it is detrimental to our well-being.

The Theory of Purpose states that "what we think we create." This means that everything that our life becomes starts with thought, whether it is positive or negative. Our conscious mind uses subconscious information to formulate thoughts and ideas, and since it is impossible to control everything we are subjected to, we must be vigilant about what we purposely feed our minds, as this will strongly influence what we consciously think, and how our lives manifest those thoughts.

There is a reason the military prefers that young people enlist. It isn't because they are generally more physically fit, but because their minds are more easily manipulated and programmed. Our conscience (or the knowing of the difference between right and wrong) sits in a part of the brain called the Ventrolateral Frontal Cortex, which is not fully developed until our early to mid-twenties. By programming young minds before their brains have fully developed, it is easier to get them to follow orders without question and even kill another human being when directed to. Right or wrong, this is done for a purpose.

We have already spoken about what happens to the body when we don't feed it proper nutrition – it gradually weakens and makes it harder to deal with stressors and live our purpose. Well, the same is true of our minds. "Garbage in, garbage out," as the saying goes. We simply cannot feed our mind with negative garbage and expect a positive outcome. Many do this, often without realizing it, and then wonder why they struggle so much. They may blame it on someone or something else, when the truth is they've turned their minds into a landfill for everything they find wrong with the world.

Be it books, movies or television, or even social media, we should find sources of positive, uplifting information and ideas with which to feed and grow our mind. Find positive, inspireational media content with high energy. Find inspirational books, listen to motivational audios, watch worthy documentaries, movies, et cetera. What we think is simply our programming, so we need to program our brain with positive thoughts and ideas so that our life reflects that.

We must also be cognizant of negative stimuli. Just as our bodies cannot tell the difference between what causes stress (real or perceived danger), our subconscious minds cannot tell the difference between reality and fantasy when it comes to negative stimuli, *even while our conscious mind is making that distinction.*

Many think the movies we watch for entertainment have no effect on us. What we don't realize is that if the movie is filled with violence or dark, negative ideas, we are feeding our subconscious this information, even if we are consciously aware that it's not reality. This "entertainment" then impacts our thoughts. Studies have borne this out. Violent video games have a negative impact on the mental health of adolescents (it affects adults as well). The problem with subjecting the mind to violent ideas and imagery on a continual basis isn't that we become more violent ourselves (although we may), but rather we become numb and indifferent to the effects of violence, so much so that when we see violence being carried out in the real world we view it with a sense of detachment and may no longer find it as shocking or abhorrent. It becomes "just the way life is."

Consider how this plays out on a daily basis. We've been programmed or conditioned to believe we live in a bad world filled with bad people. Even religions have programmed us to believe humans are sinful by nature. From our programming we could focus solely on the negative, the bad people and bad things that happen, but that doesn't make it *our* reality unless we think and believe it to be so. We can equally be programmed to think the world is a beautiful place filled with wonderful people. If our purpose is to manifest God in all we do, which serves our purpose, what will you choose to feed your mind with? How much do you love yourself?

We know that purpose is fluid and ever-changing and does so as we change. If we wish to fulfill our purpose, then we need to ask ourselves what kind of change we want to make in our life. If we wish to grow into higher levels of purpose, any change must begin with what we program our mind with.

We can't say we want our life to be one way but live it another way. Therefore, we can't say we desire happiness and then fill our minds with unhappy stimuli, no matter what its source is. Our lives will always reflect what we think. What we put into our mind has a way of finding its way back out into our reality. No one is immune to this.

So, in addition to the books and movies mentioned above, I suggest that we seek out positive people, situations, and events and, as much as we can, filter out the negative ones. Over time, we will see the results of our positive thinking. We will meet more positive people, and those who are negative will have little to no effect on us. We will encounter more positive situations that are to our benefit. We will begin to see our belief that the world is beautiful reflected back to us in the form of physical evidence, and as we imagine a world more aligned with our positive thoughts and beliefs, our life will become this way as well. If we give our brain a healthy diet of positive influence, it will drop the pounds of unwanted negativity, much like our body responds to a healthy diet.

A healthy body and mind are the foundation for a strong physical being that assists us as we serve our purpose. Now we can begin to work on transforming our life in a meaningful and lasting way. The best way to begin this journey is by learning to simply "be."

Chapter Twenty-Three

SOLITUDE AND THE
SOUND OF SILENCE

When you encounter peace and quiet, do you find it uncomfortable or disturbing, like you need to fill the void with some sound or activity? Spending time with ourselves in total silence is an absolute necessity to becoming inspired. To be inspired is to be *in-spirit*.

I've come to understand that most people cannot tolerate total silence. Not only do they need to surround themselves with some kind of sound, they cannot stand being alone with themselves. As this is the most effective way to connect with God (or this living energy of the Universe), if we cannot (or, more likely, will not) learn to sit in total solitude and silence, inspiration will continue to elude us. The space of solitude and silence is where we begin to know our true selves and, there-fore, where our purpose lies.

Prior to the rise of the industrial and technological revo-lutions, people lived infinitely quieter lives. The only sounds were those of nature, which we were much in tune with and thus more in spirit, in connection with the Universe itself. Industry gave rise to machinery and technology filled us with never-ending sources of noise, to the point that one can hardly escape it. We no longer appreciate silence, nor do we understand its benefits.

Those of you who do embrace those moments of pure silence and solitude know all too well how addictive it can be. Like any addiction, you find yourself craving it more. You are also more aware of how much noise surrounds you. You realize that even in your quietest moments, like when you're lying in bed at night, there is ALWAYS some noise going on, be it the hum of the fan or cars driving by on a nearby street, the rainfall on our roof, or even a slight breeze blowing through the leaves on trees. What you may not realize is that even these subtle and arguably benign noises interfere with and even prevent our spiritual connection, like the static on our radio when we're trying to listen to a song.

Just like light pollution has robbed us of the ability to look out into the vastness of space, noise pollution has robbed us of the ability to commune with God in silence. This communion is essential if we are to be truly inspired to live our purpose. There is a time for the sounds of nature, for music, and interaction with our fellow humans, but we must carve out time for silence as well, ideally each and every day.

From a scientific standpoint, silence is a necessity as it helps to grow new brain cells and stronger connections of neurons and synaptic fibers. Silence literally grows our brain. That alone tells us how important it is to our well-being.

We now live in a world of sensory overload and are so chronically overstimulated that we've come to believe we can't live without such stimulation. We feel we must have some background noise, something to drown out the things in life we hate. Some people can't even fall asleep without the aid of some background noise, even if it's just those machines that play the sounds of thunderstorms or birds chirping. We've been conditioned to rely on noise to function. Silence and solitude make us feel like something is missing, and in this we are correct, for in these moments what is missing is distraction!

The first time I experienced total silence was on one of my hiking trips. I had always loved hiking alone out in the wilderness. As mentioned above, this doesn't guarantee silence as even the slightest breeze rustles leaves and creates noise, subtle and pleasant as it might be. Even on a totally windless day, the activity of animals creates sound.

On one particular trip out west, I was hiking the Wonderland Trail around Mt. Rainier, a ninety-three-mile-long trail around the mountain. It is a spectacularly majestic, overwhelmingly beautiful and serene hike. It was quiet, but by no means silent.

I was, as I recall, about forty-five miles or so into the day's hike and was half-hiking and half-rock-climbing my way up the side of the mountain. I was quite high up above the alpine region where I'd left all signs of life behind. There were no trees, shrubs, grass or moss, no vegetation whatsoever. There were no animals, birds or even insects. The entire surface and surroundings were totally void of any signs of life, and the ground below me was smothered in the ash from the eruption of Mt. Saint Helens in 1980. I felt as if I were hiking on the Moon. Just one small step for me, but a giant leap for my perspective.

I stopped dead in my tracks and tried to ascertain what I was experiencing. There was no wind to stir anything. It was just me, standing alone on rock and ash, with a totally clear sky above. Then it hit me. Silence. Deafening silence. I even had to stop breathing to take it in completely. Never had I experienced such glorious beauty in my life. I was totally within myself, so deep that I lost my humanness and for the first time felt a complete connection and oneness with the Universe. It was powerfully mind-altering. It was only then that I truly understood the power of solitude and silence.

We all need solitude and silence to grow our brain and reconnect our true self, in spirit, back to God. This is where our purpose lives. People frequently tell me they don't have the time, but they think nothing of wasting precious minutes and hours on television, social media and other trivialities. We must make a commitment to finding the time for silence and solitude, even if it's only a few moments. We will soon find we crave these moments, and eventually they will become as necessary to our day as eating or sleeping.

It is with this understanding of the importance of solitude and silence that I'm giving you your first assignment. At the end of this chapter I want you to put this book down and not pick it up again for one full week. I know you might have the urge to turn the page and keep reading, but please DO NOT read past this chapter until you've completed the assignment. I want you to fully understand what happens to you in this experience. For those who have never experienced silence on purpose, this can be an invaluable lesson!

For the next week, I want you to carve out a ten-minute block of time, first thing in the morning. Set a timer for ten minutes and sit in total silence (or as close to total silence as you can possibly make it) for this amount of time. Do nothing, just sit there and pay close attention to everything, including any sounds you do hear, but most importantly to your thoughts and feelings. Once you have completed this assignment you may start reading the next chapter.

Chapter Twenty-Four

THE SOUND OF SILENCE – REVISITED

Welcome back! Knowing human behavior as I do, I'm guessing that a good number of you didn't make it through an entire week before picking this book back up. In fact, some of you probably never put it down at all. But some surely followed the assignment and hopefully reaped the enormous benefits of it. If so, congratulations!

Now that you've spent a week sitting in solitude and silence for ten minutes each day, I want you to answer a few questions. Be honest with yourself. There is no point in not being honest, because you will only be cheating yourself. It's your life, and you will only get out of it what you put into it. This is not a test, but an opportunity to contemplate and find meaning in your experience.

First, were you able to do it? By that, I mean did you start each morning (first thing) by setting aside ten minutes solely for the express purpose of sitting idle, in solitude and silence?

I know how hard it can be to break our morning routine and habits, even for a seemingly simple task such as this. Maybe it was easy for you, and if so you've made a great start to creating the change you want. If you found any part of this assignment difficult, or skipped a day, or did it later, or couldn't do it for the full ten minutes, I want you to consider just how much you want to change your life, and how willing you are to commit to it. How much do you love yourself? Your commitment serves your purpose. Spending some time in solitude and silence serves your purpose. Loving yourself serves your purpose. Doing this exercise expresses your commitment to loving yourself, and therefore to your purpose.

Now think about how you felt the very first time you sat alone in total solitude and silence. Did those ten minutes feel like an eternity? Did you peek at the timer to see how much time was left? Did you wonder what this was supposed to accomplish? Did it make you feel unsettled or anxious? Were you fidgety, or could you remain calm and relaxed? Did you fall asleep? Were you concerned about interruptions? I want you to explore the feelings you had during those ten minutes because they can give you clues as to how both silence and noise affects you.

I know from my own experience, as well as that of my clients, that most people who do this for the first time feel quite anxious and unsettled. They aren't used to silence or doing absolutely nothing. They're not used to being alone with themselves. Let's face it, we lead hectic lives, frantically bouncing from one thing to the next like busy little squirrels. Idleness is frowned upon. We've been programmed to always stay busy doing something, anything, so we can accomplish things, even if they are trivial in nature. We are programmed to always be doing something, as just "being" is a waste of precious time. This thinking and behavior is a clear sign of the Material level of purpose.

You might be thinking that there is no reason to spend ten minutes in silence when you get more than that when you are sleeping. But silence and solitude are a completely different experience when you are fully awake and aware of it. You must be in a conscious state of mind so that you can tap into the divinity of your life, for this is where purpose lies, in the seat of your connection to the Consciousness of the Universe.

As awareness in the *what we do* is necessary, I want you to consider whether you were actually in *total* silence. Were you able to perceive any subtle sounds you normally aren't aware of? Maybe your furnace or air conditioner kicked in while you were doing this exercise. Perhaps you heard the creaks and groans of your house settling, or you heard yourself shifting your position in the chair, or maybe the sound of the wind or traffic outside could be heard. How many sounds were audible, if only barely perceptible? There is more noise around us than we are aware of and this experiment proves this to be true. Unless you were in a sensory deprivation chamber, or wore ear plugs or noise-canceling headphones, chances are you were not in total silence. If this was the case, I suggest obtaining some ear plugs or headphones for the future. The point is, silence is a different experience when you can immerse yourself in it completely.

If you were able to block out all noise, were you aware of the sound of your breathing? It was there even if you didn't notice it. But even in the sound of your breathing, there is something else that is extremely difficult to ignore. It's a different sound, and it isn't one your ears can physically detect. Did you notice it? What was it?

In these ten minutes of silence, did you happen to hear the voice in your head? You know the voice I'm talking about, because it never stops talking to you. That's your ego, and I bet it never shut up the entire time you were sitting there. I'm also pretty sure of what it said, things like, *"What was that sound? Oh God, I feel uneasy...I hate just sitting here! Why are we doing this? When is that timer going to go off? I should check to see how much time has passed. Do I really need to do this? I have to get ready for work. I know I'm supposed to do this for ten minutes, but I've done it long enough. I'll do ten minutes tomorrow. How much time is left? Really? Only five minutes have gone by?"* On and on it went, narrating your solitude and interrupting your efforts to connect with your true self and the Divine.

Every single thought we have is expressed by our ego; it fills our head with so much chatter about our current reality (based on past experience) that sitting in silence is almost impossible. Perhaps your ears didn't hear it, but I know YOU did. The real you. The one that hears the voice. The ego won't allow you to be in spirit, to just *be*. We need to learn how to shut that voice up. We need to quiet the ego and free up some mind space. Silence may be golden, but quieting the ego is priceless.

In this next chapter we will learn how to quiet the ego, and learn to be truly still, in solitude and silence, where we can make that connection to God. In the meantime, keep doing your ten minutes of solitude and silence every morning. It will pay off once it becomes a habit. You will learn to enjoy it and want it, if not need it. We will use this solitude and silence to further our growth by using some techniques that can take us to another level of purpose.

Chapter Twenty-Five

MEDITATION IS NOT
A ZEN THING

Now that you have experienced solitude and silence, you might have discovered something about the world around you (and within) that you were not previously aware of. You've discovered that in addition to the external noises, we also have to deal with the incessant chatter of the voice in our head. Thus we are never living in total silence. That does not mean, however that the time spent in silence and solitude was futile; in fact it has already taught the first of many valuable lessons.

Were you aware of that voice prior to this exercise? Did it even cross your mind that you are always talking to yourself? Now that you've experienced it, are you more aware of it? Do you now find that voice almost annoying you? This was my experience when I first discovered this voice for myself. It had never bothered me before, but once I was aware, it became an intrusion — constantly narrating my life and providing a running commentary on *everything*. As discussed in a previous chapter, this voice is not you talking to you. It is your ego talking to the real you, restating your current reality based solely on your programmed past.

In that first exercise of solitude, the voice in your head was a major distraction. Did you find yourself paying so much attention to that voice that you didn't really appreciate the solitude? In order to be open and to have true spirit-awareness we need to quiet the ego's voice. We need to control when and how it is able to talk to us and, eventually, to prevent it from being there at all. Meditation is a tool used just for this purpose.

There are so many misconceptions about meditation. Just hearing the term conjures up a picture of some Zen Buddhist yogi sitting atop a mountain in the lotus position, a cloud of burning incense surrounding him as he chants "Om" over and over again. In truth, meditation is nothing more than a stillness, a calm, a way of just "being" rather than "doing." It isn't limited to any one religion or philosophy, and though we could consider it a form of prayer (without words or thought), it is available to all, even atheists.

Meditation, in its simplest and purest form, is the practice of letting go. We let go of thought, of words, of activity (both physical and mental) and most importantly, we let go of the ego that controls us.

Meditation is also the art of breathing. I could write an entire book on the benefits of breathwork, and most of us have tried to calm ourselves or someone else down by saying, "Just breathe." At any given moment we can pause, take a deep breath, and notice how frantic our lives really are. Most everything we do is based in that egoic voice in our head, making us feel like we must keep moving, thinking, talking and acting. Meditation, which includes placing our focus on the breath, is the practice we use to remove the ego, return to our true selves and to the divine.

"The Tao does nothing but leaves nothing undone.
If powerful men could center themselves in it
the whole world would be transformed by itself,
in its natural rhythms.
When life is simple,
pretenses fall away;
our essential natures shine through.
By not wanting, there is calm,
and the world will straighten itself.
When there is silence,
one finds the anchor of the universe within oneself."

In this thirty-seventh verse of the *Tao Te Ching*, Lao Tsu encourages us to just "be," and in our being, where we are doing nothing, nothing is left undone. We are expressing pure purpose, in love with the process of our breathing and being; our *natural rhythm*. In this connection to the Consciousness of the Universe (God or the Tao) our purpose is manifested not by *what* we are doing or *why*, but in *how* we are engaging with life. In this case, there is no action; our "work" here, if you will, is to release the ego, and return to our spiritual state of mind where *life is simple* and *pretenses fall away; our essential natures shine through.* While in this meditative state, the chaos of the mind and ego, our internal world, can be at rest.

Many of my clients don't initially understand meditation and have no idea how to practice it. They attempt it, and often come to their next session telling me that they must be doing it wrong, or that they struggled with it. Let me assure you that there really is no right or wrong way to meditate, save for the fact that if you're struggling you most assuredly are not meditating. Meditation is the exact opposite of struggle. It is the release of struggle. Meditation is the act of letting everything go.

Breathing is a key component of meditation. It is just so natural, and we do so without thought because breathing *is living*. In settling ourselves, quieting the ego and just being, the act of breathing allows us to let go of everything but life itself. Meditation is you, your breathing and God. That's it, and it is enough. It is our ego that demands there be more.

What other activity have you ever engaged in that allowed you to just let everything go? I'm sure it's happened, perhaps without you even realizing it. Have you ever laid on a beach in the warm sun, peacefully knowing that you weren't required to do anything other than soak up the rays? Well, that's almost meditation! This and other activities are available to us each day, but we must make time for them rather than relegating them to dreams of weekends, vacations and retirement.

In the previous exercise I asked you to find some time, first thing in the morning, to be in solitude and silence. Now we are going to build upon that foundation by adding meditation.

First, find a comfortable sitting position. To be most beneficial, you should be upright, with correct but relaxed posture. Don't slouch, but don't force yourself out of being relaxed either. You want to be in a position that allows good blood flow to your entire body, so eliminate any position or external things in your surroundings that constrict your body and instead use things like comfortable furniture and pillows, wear loose clothing, et cetera. You want to be completely relaxed, but not so much that you fall asleep.

Once you are in a comfortable, relaxed position, start your timer for ten minutes and close your eyes. Breathe. While breathing is an automatic body function done without conscious thought, in meditation we want to focus and increase our awareness of it. I want you to be so attentive to your breathing that it becomes your sole focus point.

Now, inhale slowly but fully to the count of five. Hold your breath to the count of five, then exhale fully to the count of five, always being conscious of your breathing and nothing else. What you will find at first is that not only are you paying attention to your breathing, you are also paying attention to your counting. Most often, at the outset you will hear that voice in your head… "One, two, three, four, five" and then your ego will jump in. *Hey, I hit the count of five but I can still inhale more! Should I inhale more, or should I start holding my breath now? Oh shoot… One, two — wait, maybe I should be exhaling by now. Dang, I lost count now and I should just start over. Am I doing this right? I don't think I am.*

See how the ego tries to take over and undermine your meditation? This is because you are so concerned with *doing it right* instead of just *being*. Just relax and start over. Don't worry about breathing so precisely to the count of five on your inhales, holding and exhales. The counting is simply to get you to breathe steadily and to be aware of it. Any thought of "how" you are breathing or counting should be dismissed instantly. Whenever a thought comes to you, let it go and return your focus to your breathing. It is always about your breathing.

Here is the best advice I can give you with regard to meditation: do not fight your ego. The moment you decide to quiet your mind, you will hear that egoic voice begin its chatter. Your natural instinct will be to fight it, but the more you try to silence these thoughts, the more they will seem to multiply and increase in volume. Though you're hopelessly outmatched, you keep fighting and before you know it you've spent the entire ten minutes battling your ego instead of connecting with God. Remember, the ego is extremely powerful. It is also deeply invested in holding you in your current reality (as it knows nothing else) and it has an arsenal of life experiences at its disposal.

Do not waste your time attempting to suppress thoughts or trying to block them from entering your mind; instead, learn to let them go. How do we do this? By simply allowing the thought to exist without fighting it or dwelling upon it. This is the "practice" part of your meditation practice. When a thought comes, acknowledge it, and then immediately go back to focusing on your breathing. More thoughts will come and, again, allow them in and refocus your attention on your breathing. If it helps, try to imagine letting your thoughts come *in during inhales* and allow them to *escape via exhales.* This will attach your thought to your breathing, which forces you to focus on your breathing.

With time and practice, you will find that the thoughts are fewer and farther between and that it's just you and your breathing. Then one day you'll realize that even your breathing isn't a part of your awareness any longer. Like my epiphany during that fateful hike, or Edgar Mitchell's savikalpa samādhi experience in space, you literally will just "be," and in just being, you will see the world and your place in it from a new perspective. Of course, you will not have that kind of experience every time you meditate, and inevitably thoughts will sneak in. Observe them, as they can offer clues as to where you are on your journey. They will also challenge your currently held beliefs and concepts, including those around time.

We've already covered how much time we waste on trivialities, even as we lament that we don't have a moment to spend on personal growth. A regular meditation practice, with all its life-affirming benefits, will make you more aware of the activities that rob you of time and prevent you from living your purpose. What I am taking about here is your concept of time itself.

Time is nothing more than a human construct, something else that is programmed into us. Even if we know this, we don't give it too much thought, until we start to meditate. In the beginning, you will be extremely conscious of every second. Ten minutes seems like an eternity, and I can almost guarantee you are going to want to peek at your timer to see if you set it properly, because you will think that surely it should have gone off by now. If you do peek, you'll be quite shocked to see that you've only been meditating for five minutes or less. But this feeling won't last.

You will find at some point that what used to feel like an eternity now feels like almost no time has passed. As you progress in your meditation practice, ten minutes will feel insufficient and you will desire even more time. In reality, you are becoming more aware of your spirit, which has no concept of time because of its eternal nature. In essence, you are, as Lao Tsu wrote, *"finding the anchor of the Universe within yourself."* As your perception of time changes, take note. This is the real you, the spiritual you, becoming more self-aware. With daily practice, you will see how this self-awareness plays out positively in your life.

In previous chapters I mentioned that there is much work to be done in order to change, that action is a part of purpose, and that we must make a commitment to take this action — yet here I tell you to sit in meditation and do nothing! This can seem like a contradiction, and to explain it I once again turn to Lao Tsu: *"The Tao does nothing, but leaves nothing undone."* Yes, we must act and there is a lot of work to be done, but meditation allows us to release ourselves from the ego and whatever control it has over us. When we do this daily, we have greater clarity of mind with which to resolve our conflicts, rather than thinking and acting from emotions and the faulty programming of our ego. It will allow us to fulfill our purpose, manifesting God in all that we do.

In addition to meditation there is another technique we can use to further purge the negativity from our life and create new, positive intentions.

Chapter Twenty-Six

WHAT'S SO RIGHT
ABOUT WRITING?

Have you ever written an angry letter (or, today, more likely an email) to someone for a real or imagined slight, only to never mail/send it? The act of writing down your feelings allows you to vent, releasing that emotion of anger, all without the recipient being aware of it. That is precisely what this next exercise is all about.

First, put any trepidations aside, because like the above example, no one will ever see what you write. This is journaling, and it is simply about writing how you feel in the moment; it is another way to release emotional and physical tension and stress. You cannot get it wrong.

There are times when we need to unload our troubles, and the simple act of talking about them allows us to release them from our mind. The problem is, this form of release can become habitual complaining, which is a *negative* way of dealing with them. Our words have power, so while giving voice to our problems might make us feel better in the moment, it is a restatement of our current reality; it also sends negative energy to whoever is listening to our complaints. As it is not constructive to suppress or deny our feelings either, we must find other outlets to express these negative emotions. Journaling is a highly cathartic and highly effective means of accomplishing this.

Journaling is also an excellent way to resolve conflict. Though contemplating conflict and attempting to find resolution within our mind is helpful, the pent-up negative energy can remain. But writing them out on paper (and I do contend that writing it out by hand is more effective than typing) engages both the mind and body, helping the energy transfer out of us and onto the page. Journaling can also help us objectively understand our internal conflicts and gain insight into our thoughts (that *"thinking about your thoughts"* mentioned previously). It can also illuminate resolutions to conflict, spark our imagination, create an idea, or give us greater clarity on many other aspects of our life.

If we pay attention, we will see immediate evidence of the benefits of journaling. As we write, we'll feel how much tension is in our body by how tightly we grip the pen or pencil, as well as how this tension fluctuates with the specific words being written. We will grip the pen tighter and possibly even cramp up when we are writing negative things, and we might feel our grip loosening as we write positive thoughts and feelings out on the paper. It is truly a remarkable tool.

As mentioned above, there really is no right or wrong way to journal, yet most of my life coaching clients struggle with it as much as they do with meditation. And like meditation, this usually passes with practice. Some don't enjoy writing; others find it uncomfortable, but this doesn't let them off the hook. There is much we must do in order to grow, little of which is pleasing because growth requires resolution to conflict. That is the point of these exercises: to develop them into daily rituals that become a part of the routine of our new growth. Developing new habits and routines creates conflict within us too. Embrace the conflict and do it anyway.

After your morning meditation, reset your timer for another ten minutes. This is the perfect time to journal, as meditation opens you up and puts you in a contemplative state, allowing you to get in touch with your thoughts and feelings on a much deeper level. Now, while in this contemplative state, begin writing whatever comes to mind, positive or negative. In this way, the practice of journaling is the opposite of meditation. Instead of allowing thoughts to simply come and go, we allow them in and then hold them long enough to write them down. The two exercises are different, yes, but they are both about release.

As you do this, you'll find that some words trigger other thoughts, so write about them too. Don't edit yourself, or obsess over how to express it, or whether the grammar or spelling is correct. Also, don't exclude any positive emotions. If you are feeling happy, grateful, excited or energized, write that down as well. In fact, you might find the one sentence is negative and the very next one is positive, your emotions ebbing and flowing with no apparent rhyme or reason. Just go with it and know that this exercise is meant to help you release your ego. Write as quickly as you can to try to keep up with the thoughts, and as you do so, pay attention to the tension in your body. Notice how it flows out of you, like pouring water out of a pitcher.

As with meditation, these ten minutes may also feel like an eternity; you may even find yourself wracking your brain for something to write about. But eventually, with daily practice, your concept of time will once again shift and the timer will go off long before you are done writing. Again, don't struggle. This is not meant to be another chore or something else you use to judge yourself with. No one is going to read it, and you can even throw away the paper afterward if you care to.

That said, there is much to be gained by keeping and

rereading our journal entries. We can easily get caught up in our flawed thinking, but when we write it out and then read what we've written, we can get a glimpse into our own being with some level of objectivity (this is even more profound when we read them again at a later date). I like to keep my journals and occasionally look back to see where I was and compare it to where I am now. I also use it as a springboard for ideas and you may as well, but for now it's simply an exercise in letting go of your deepest thoughts and feelings, no matter what they are.

More than anything, journaling is a way of communicating with yourself. You can even allow your ego to do all the talking if you want to. Though it is babbling on like it always does, the act of writing it down allows you to let those thoughts go without causing harm. Moreover, it can help you become more aware of just how much of your thought comes from the ego and past programming. You might possibly learn a lesson, find some answer you seek or a way to set new positive intentions. In meditation you find your true self, and in journaling you lose your false self. When combined together daily, over time, you will begin seeing positive results showing up as you go about living with purpose.

Now set your timer and start writing! Have fun with this! It can be an enjoyable exercise.

Chapter Twenty-Seven

AFFIRM THE POSITIVE WITH GRATITUDE

The practices of meditation and journaling are simple but excellent tools to help us quiet the ego, release negativity and create a positive mindset. Once we open ourselves and release the mental toxins, we now must reset our thinking, program new thought and direct our attention to all that is positive. Again, the best way to accomplish this is by setting intentions and continuing to mind our thoughts and beliefs. In this future life we will create, we should be grateful for everything, not only past and present, but even those things that haven't manifested *yet.* How can we express gratitude for that which we do not yet possess? Affirmations.

Don't think of affirmations as a "pep talk" to convince yourself. Doing so will render them useless. Their purpose lies not in convincing us of an alternative to our current reality, but rather to overwrite our existing programming with one that will now serve our purpose. Science has proven that the synapses of our brain are wired in a particular manner, for the neurons to travel and operate as we direct them. As we create negative thought, positive synapses detach and become replaced with negative connections. The longer we hold negative thought, the more synapses are created to support them. Likewise, positive thought makes positive connections. Affirmations help us literally rewire our brains to function with new, positive thought.

Back in the "olden days," telephone operators had to physically plug in phone lines to make connections that enabled us to communicate with one another. Once a call was completed, the operator would then unplug that line so it could be used for another call. This is exactly how our brains work. We have thoughts that require the line of communication to be connected. It then travels through this connection for us to function. The more "phone calls" of thought we place, the more connections there are. Now consider how our thoughts place these calls. If you want to create your life, do you want to place positive or negative calls? You have the ability to tell the "operator" in your brain to connect you to the positive or the negative. Whatever choice you make, the operator will oblige you every time. Obviously, the best choice is to wire your brain to make as many positive connections as possible. The more positive synapses you create the more positive your "calls" will turn out to be.

Recall that in the chapter on the ego, it can only playback what was recorded (or programmed) into it. However, affirmations stated in the present are like recording over the ego's programming of the past, creating a new playback that is positive and uplifting about our future.

Affirmations also serve as reminders not to be lazy in our thought; if we are, we will be subjected to "random" occurrences, not to mention the whims of others. In creating affirmations, we not only need to be specific as to what we want, we must direct these thoughts in the most positive way possible, leaving no doubt as to our intentions. We cannot be vague with our intentions, any more than we would want the phone operator to place random phone calls for us. Be sure of your intended connections with your affirmations and what will manifest is *exactly what you already affirm to be true.* Affirmations are the expression of our intentions. We can think of them as leading our purpose.

Before I return to setting specific intentions with your affirmations, I must turn to the crucial component of gratitude. It is with gratitude that all things come into existence. As mentioned above, we must be grateful for everything we have and everything we are (both good and bad), as well as everything we wish to be. It might seem counterproductive to be grateful for the bad things that have happened to us, but let's remember the duality of life and how good/bad are really the same thing, with only our perspective making it one way or the other. You must view every bad situation you've ever found yourself in with gratitude, for it is in these circumstances that life offers us lessons, via conflict, to resolve. Just as sadness allows us to know happiness, and illness affords gratitude for being healthy, we must see past the bad and look to the lesson within it. Be grateful for that lesson. See all future circumstances in this light.

When you infuse your affirmations with gratitude, they take on new meaning and have more power and positive energy associated with them. With gratitude your affirmations are less about convincing yourself and more about the absolute belief in your statements, because you already know them to be true. This is where your intentions take shape. You state your affirmations as truths, be they truth about the gratitude of your past, your present or your future. So, what does that future hold? It's your future you are creating, so be specific as to what your truth will be.

Just as what we think we create, what we *believe* we *attract.* Affirmations are affirming or acknowledging *the convictions of our beliefs.* The depth of your belief in what you affirm to be true is what gives affirmations power. When you affirm, "I am healthy," especially when your current state may show evidence to the contrary, it is your *belief* that *you will be healthy*. Affirmations without belief are empty attempts at convincing, whereas with the backing of your belief, they state *how things will be* as a matter of fact.

Affirmations are the Law of Attraction in action. The depth of your belief is shown by the actions you take to make what you affirm possible. When your beliefs are strong, they carry with them great feelings or emotions. It is with these feelings that your beliefs have their strongest energy. As was mentioned in the chapter about the Law of Attraction, you can't simply affirm something to be true and then sit around waiting for it to happen; you have to take action. When you believe in something with conviction, the more action you will take to make it so.

Be careful with how you affirm all that you are currently grateful for and all you intend to be grateful for in your future. Never use negative statements. For example, we may be overweight, and in our gratitude for the lesson we learned from being overweight (i.e. being sick, uncomfortable, having low self-esteem, et cetera) we express our affirmation and state it in a specific positive manner. For example, "I AM healthy and at my ideal weight which will bring me continued health and well-being." Never state it negatively like, "I am tired of being fat and sick and I wish I weren't overweight." You may very well be sick and tired of being overweight, but DO NOT state it this way in your affirmation. You must have the thought in your mind that you are *already at your ideal weight and healthy*. Do you see the difference? Everything in our affirmations must state what we desire, in the most specific, positive way possible, leaving nothing to chance, or to the "accidental" interpretation of the ego.

"I AM" statements like the one above make excellent affirmations, for they exclaim our intentions to the Universe. Whatever I AM statement we make will become manifested in our future reality. Making these statements now, even in the absence of evidence, demonstrates the strength of our belief that we will see it as our truth in some future moment in time. Our current reality came about in this manner, except we most likely created it mindlessly. Now is the time to be aware and mindful about our intentions as we move forward.

Thus, we state our affirmations about our future as positive statements of fact. This is the very nature of inspired creation and the Law of Attraction. If you want to change your future, you can't rely on your current reality to determine it. See your future life in your mind's eye, as this beautiful creation already completed. See it from the perspective of the real you, the spirit you, that simultaneously exists in the past, present and future. Once you know this future to be true in your mind, you direct your intentions to making it so. Remember, per the Theory of Purpose, *what we think, we create.*

This is the essence of your next exercise. After you have finished your previous exercises, set your timer for another ten minutes and begin stating your affirmations. You can either write or say them, whichever works best for you. Make present-tense statements of gratitude for absolutely anything and everything you can think of, past, present and future. For example, "I AM grateful for all that has taken place that allowed me to learn and grow"; "I AM grateful to have this day with which to live out my purpose"; "I AM grateful for my job, my family, my friends"; "I AM happy"; "I AM healthy"; "I AM at my ideal weight"; " I AM beautiful"; "I AM creative"; "I AM living life with purpose, fulfillment and meaning."

As was mentioned previously, we can use the Six Elements of Life to set our intentions. Look over those categories again, set some intentions specific to each one, and create affirmations stating those intentions as if they have already manifested. As you have already identified weak areas in the PIE questionnaire, you can use these affirmations to help you to grow.

As with the meditation and journaling exercises, there is no right or wrong way to do this, so long as you state your affirmations in the positive, with gratitude and backed by your absolute belief that they are true. Make a commitment to do this each and every day, as the third segment of your morning practice. We are building a new life and so we must create a new routine filled with these positive habits. Do so out of Love for yourself, and in time you will begin to see your life change. These changes might be grand, or they might be subtle. You might find yourself becoming happier, or perhaps calmer and at peace. You may start to attract the very things you've needed to express your purpose. We can't always know how or when these things will manifest, but the Universe will provide them (as needed) at the perfect time and place. Be grateful for that.

Chapter Twenty-Eight

THE DREAMER

Children are in tune with their true, spiritual nature. Playing and dreaming is instinctual, without anyone having to teach them how to do it. Out of this natural instinct comes the need to explore and discover. But this process of discovery, playing and dreaming gets interrupted by the programming of our society. The ability to dream is essentially programmed out of us until we no longer have a dream or purpose worth pursuing. Without purpose our lives have no meaning, and without meaning we live our lives solely in pursuit of material objects and/or out of obligations to others. We live our lives on autopilot and wonder why we are unfulfilled. As mentioned earlier, this is the entry level of Materialism, and without dreams we may remain there for the rest of our lives. But how, after years of stagnation, can we reignite our imagination and visualize a different life?

This is where the Theory of Purpose comes in. Remember way back in the third chapter, when you completed the PIE (Purpose Inventory Evaluation)? Well, grab a pen and your paper and let us revisit the five life categories.

In this exercise, we are going to dare to dream again. We are going to visualize this new life, our new purpose, in order to create and fulfill them. I want you to look at your answers and see where you thought you were putting the priority and intention for your life as it stands currently. Now we are going to go through this list again, but instead of seeing *where we are*, we are going to visualize *where we want to be*.

As you look at each category, see yourself in the future, living your ideal life. Close your eyes and picture this ideal life with regard to that particular category. What do you see? Fill out a new sheet, not with your old answers, but with this new dream of your life. Express how much Love you will have for yourself.

Physical and Mental Health —
> **What** am I doing with this part of my life?
> **How** am I working on it?
> **Why** am I doing it?

Jobs or Careers and Finance —
> **What** am I doing with this part of my life?
> **How** am I working on it?
> **Why** am I doing it?

Relationships —
> **What** am I doing with this part of my life?
> **How** am I working on it?
> **Why** am I doing it?

Religious or Spiritual Beliefs —
> **What** am I doing with this part of my life?
> **How** am I working on it?
> **Why** am I doing it?

Personal Growth —
> **What** am I doing with this part of my life?
> **How** am I working on it?
> **Why** am I doing it?

This exercise is the perfect tool to set your affirmations. You can state them as such:

I AM physically and mentally healthy.

I AM working in a career I find rewarding and fulfilling.
I AM in healthy and loving relationships.
I AM in connection with God daily.
I AM enlightened, manifesting God in all that I do.
I AM Love.

Now that you have filled in these categories with a new perception of how you imagine your life being, I want you to again set your timer for ten minutes, just as you did with the previous exercises, and go through this list every morning, visualizing each category as if you already are living them in this new way. This is the visualization exercise and you must do it every morning. What you imagine you become. Imagine loving everything about yourself in this new life.

Chapter Twenty-Nine

HABITS BECOME LIFESTYLE

Anything we do with repetition eventually becomes habit, especially when done at the same time every day. The longer and more consistently we do anything the more we reinforce the habit. Habits are automatic actions. The Theory of Purpose states, "What we think, *we create*. What we believe, *we attract*. What we imagine, *we become*." If you want to live with purpose, these ideas, and the new exercises you are developing, must become routine and habitual as part of your new lifestyle.

To recap, your morning routine now consists of doing these four things, ten minutes each, as soon as you wake up.

Meditation — Use this to release the ego and negative energy, and restore your connection to spirit, which is your true, eternal being.

Journaling — Use this to release pent-up emotional negative energy, both physical and mental, but also to send out and create positive energy and ideas.

Affirmations — Use these to declare to the Consciousness of the Universe (or God) what you desire and what you believe that your life will be from now on.

Visualization (Dreaming) — Use this to imagine this future life you will have with great clarity and belief. Picture it in your mind as if you already have it, as what you imagine you *will* become.

Reminding ourselves of this new lifestyle is a great way to reprogram our thoughts and beliefs, so tell yourself a new story. Read this story below as if you are already living it.

"My daily routine now consists of high energy, positive thinking, so I routinely feed my mind with positive influences in all I think, say, and do. I engage in reading, watching, or listening to content filled with positive messages, and remove all negative content and imagery from my life, be it entertainment or toxic relationships.

I've changed my lifestyle and now enjoy a healthy diet with exercise. I am grateful for everything in my current reality, be it good or bad. In the good, I find joy and express gratitude, but I'm also grateful for the bad and now see it as coming into my life as a lesson to be learned, a conflict that is understood for its purpose. I resolve it and let it go.

With every person and situation I encounter, I recognize my emotional reaction and embrace it, feeling it fully, and then let it go, not allowing my emotions to control me but rather using my thought to keep my emotions under control. I now know that I cannot change people or the world around me in order to be okay. I change myself and how I choose to react.

I set my intentions every morning to create the life I desire, and then go out and live this new life each and every day as if it were my current reality, fully conscious of the fact that I alone create my life, attracting all the people and circumstances into it in order to grow. I am mindful of the life I am living as I live it, as this is living on purpose and being in the present moment.

I seek purpose each day, always asking myself who I am and why I am here and searching for the answers to these eternal questions. I promise myself to always strive to live in spirit and in Love, silencing the ego that used to run my life. In this way I find joy, peace, contentment and fulfillment, thereby living a meaningful life.

I put into action the Theory of Purpose, which is stated personally by me:

'My purpose is not a singularity, but the fluid, ongoing experiential process of my life. I AM the manifestation of the Consciousness of the Universe, co-creating and manifesting my life into existence. What I think I create. What I believe I attract. What I imagine I become. My thoughts, beliefs and imagination set my intention. In my intention, I express my purpose, manifesting my experience. My experience creates conflict and through its resolution I will achieve growth, which provides contextual meaning for my life. My shared, universal purpose is Love, yet I uniquely express it individually, as a manifestation of the Consciousness of the Universe.'"

This is the story we can tell ourselves, replacing our old thoughts and beliefs with this new way of being. It can be thought of as a mindful meditation or prayer of how we want to live our life. This can be your story if you want it to be, no matter what has gone on before.

In all that we do, we can remind ourselves of our purpose by asking, "How does this serve my purpose?" or "How does this manifest God?" We can diligently be mindful of our purpose. Remember, mindfulness is *paying attention to our intentions.* If we want to create the life we imagine, we must always practice the art of being mindful *in everything we do.* We set our intentions and then we *pay attention to stay on task to ensure we make it happen.* That is mindfulness and commitment. We aren't going to be consistently mindful all the time, but if we strive to remain aware, over time this *practice* will become *habit* and, eventually, second nature — our new way of living.

If we put forth the actions outlined in this book regularly, and then mindfully live from our spirit state, our life *will* change. Time will appear to slow down and peace will envelope us. We will love ourselves more deeply and fully, accepting our perceived flaws as "perfection in our imperfection." This new way of living will seem like a dream because it really is; it's the one we imagined. This is the alternate reality of our own creation.

Chapter Thirty

OUR PURPOSE –
THE ALTERNATE REALITY

"I am he as you are he as you are me, and we are all together."
~ John Lennon

We truly are all one. Not just one with each other, but with all that exists. The same living energy that created the Universe, created you. You are a beautiful person. Everything about you radiates this beauty. Within you lies the limitless potential and energy to be everything you wish to be, to make your dreams come true, and to share them with the world. I don't have to meet you to know you. I am you and you are me. Within you also lives an artist, with the capacity and ability to create the most beautiful work of art in existence: your life.

When I look out into space, I see the ever-expanding Universe and I lose myself in it. It is in losing myself that I find my true being. I look out at countless galaxies, nebulae and clusters of stars among billions and billions of others we have yet to discover, and it makes me contemplate my existence. I see other worlds far beyond our own and wonder if life exists out there as well. In such an expansive Universe what grand purpose could we ever serve? We are at once nothing and everything, solely because we are conscious of our existence. But where does this consciousness come from? What gave us this awareness?

This Universe reminds me to always look at the bigger picture. My life, even taken as a whole, is still of such insignificance. I am but a singular speck of an idea born out of this Universe, created out of the same material, the same energy of all that exists. So I wonder, *Why?*

When I think of my life in the context of this grand Universe, it changes my perspective. I lose my labels, my identity, my humanness. I see myself not as me, but as a part of the entire Universe. I see myself in this big picture of all that is. This prompts me to ask the two universal questions that we should all contemplate as we live out this experience we call life:

Who am I?

Why am I here?

While we all seek to improve our own individual lives, it is important to put our lives in the context of the Universe; otherwise, life has no real meaning. Personal growth is nothing more than our individual progress. It is only about ourselves, being selfishly aware that we seek to become more than we are. Yet, what are we? To what grand purpose does our own purpose *in being* serve?

If we do not attempt to answer those two questions above, then I question why we even need to exist at all. Surely there is more to our existence than this chaotic, random life we are all living. We can't possibly exist for the express purpose of acquiring material wealth. The meaning of our existence cannot be defined solely by how much money we have, or the homes we live in, or the careers we have. It cannot be to secure our own happiness at the expense of others or the planet itself.

So what is the reason for our existence? Why be born at all if the only thing we end up doing is dying anyway? What then is the big deal with what we do in between birth and death?

Einstein proposed that everything in existence is either energy or mass, both equally interchangeable. If we *only* see ourselves in the context of our physical bodies, then nothing about our existence is justified. But, if we can see our spirits as *energy* and our bodies as *mass*, then for our spirit to fully experience the physical world we must become mass ourselves. When our bodies cease to exist, or when we are done with the experience, we go back to being pure spirit or energy again.

If we can look at our life in this context, then we can change our perspective and shift it towards an alternate idea as to who we are. If we are spirit, then life takes on an entirely different meaning than when we think of ourselves as bodies serving no purpose to the Universe. As spirits we can think of ourselves as beings of energy that experience the Universe on the physical plane, thus eternal as energy, but temporal as mass. This eternal energy can be expressed as God, our source of existence, or the Consciousness of the Universe itself.

In this way, the more fully we experience life the more purpose we have for existing. We are the expression or *manifestation* of the Consciousness of the living Universe. The I AM.

So in answering the first question — "Who am I?" — the only answer is "I AM"; no other qualifier is required because anything added is a limitation. When Jesus was asked if he was God, he simply answered, "I AM," and that was sufficient. He was stating that he was an eternal manifestation of God, or the Consciousness of the Universe. When you can answer that question with the same confident "I AM," you will have discovered your true self. And, when you can answer the question — "Why am I here?" — with "For the Consciousness of the Universe (God) to fully experience itself," you will know why you exist. You will be stating this is why I AM conscious of my existence. I AM the very manifestation of Consciousness itself.

What gives meaning to our existence is *experiencing* our self. We cannot experience our self through others; we can only do that through the life we create, just as the Consciousness of the Universe, or God, experiences itself through the life it creates. This is the true "circle of life," each experiencing life through our creation of it, serving the purpose of each other, which gives meaning to our existence. It is in our experience that the Consciousness of the Universe manifested us. This is why we exist.

Manifest God in all that you do, do it all out of Love, and you will have discovered your purpose.

ABOUT THE AUTHOR

*M*ark Mittlesteadt is a father, teacher, life coach, author, artist, musician, astronomer and a spiritual practitioner in the Taoist/Buddhist traditions. He discovered his purpose in life from a transformative experience in childhood. He realized at a very young age that he understood the world on a deeper level than his contemporaries. Though he did not understand the meaning until many years later, it was through these experiences that led him to follow his passions and become an artist, musician and writer. Mark has devoted his life to the exploration of beauty, meaning and purpose.

In his early twenties he studied to become a minister, but after becoming frustrated by the dogmatic ideologies of religion, he set out to uncover truth wherever it was to be found. He has spent his life on a journey of self-discovery, be it backpacking trips out in the wilderness to commune with nature; his study of the Universe through astronomy; contemplating our existence in scientific and religious contexts; finding beauty and truth through his creative endeavors; or learning to apply the scientific principles of psychology to the human condition.

Mark has been a professional artist for more than forty years, painting every subject in every medium for a wide variety of clients, and his work is in private and public collections around the world. He devoted two years of his life exclusively to creating the one-of-a-kind "Wild Wisconsin" natural history museum for the DC Everest School District's environmental center in central Wisconsin, incorporating murals and dioramas and using taxidermy mounts to depict animals in their natural habitats.

Mark has also explored another aspect of the arts as a copywriter and author. He served as ghostwriter for a thrilling biography of a man immersed in the life of Mexican drug cartels and the mafia. He also co-authored and illustrated *Rocky the Rock Bass and the Jammin' Minnows,* a children's book about discovering and fulfilling purpose.

In the 1990s, at the height of his career as an artist, he began conducting the unique "Artist Within" workshops to teach other artists his methods for discovering meaning and purpose in life and how to then express it in their own art. He essentially became a "life coach" before there was a term for it.

For as much success as he has enjoyed throughout his life, Mark acknowledges that his life was not always one of joy and success. He also discovered that it is in working through the many failures that we learn the most about life. Through his own struggle with depression, failed relationships, divorce, and a myriad of other experiences we all may go through, it was his never-ending, undying spiritual quest to find meaning and fulfillment in his purpose that he eventually learned to heal and love himself again. He remarried and raised four children. Two of his children battled addiction and this experience led Mark to return to college late in life and study psychology, attempting to understand the science behind why we think and act the way we do.

While Mark has studied human behavior throughout his life, his formal education in psychology allowed him to see the human condition in a new way. Mark's experience and education in the arts and sciences allows him to work with others who struggle with life in unique, creative and imaginative ways.

His method of counseling is a blend of modern psychological therapies combined with the Eastern traditions in spirituality and energy. This is what sparked the idea of what is now known as his "Theory of Purpose," which this book is based upon. Through his teachings and coaching practice, he has returned full circle, back to becoming the minister he wanted to be, showing others how to love and live with purpose.

He teaches his clients how to love themselves and to think of purpose in an entirely new way so that it can be expressed fully on a daily basis. Like an alchemist, his clients learn to utilize the elements of the Theory of Purpose to create the life they dream of — one with limitless possibilities and endless Love.

How to Connect with Mark Mittlesteadt

You can follow Mark Mittlesteadt and connect with him via his website, www.the-artist-within.com, and social media platforms like Facebook and LinkedIn. Mark works with clients all around the world via phone, e-mail, video conferencing and in person through lectures, workshops and personal counseling sessions. Mark also regularly posts new blogs on his website.

By becoming a member of The Artist Within community, you'll be able to access Mark's blogs, view and purchase his artwork, see upcoming scheduled events, and be an active participant on his Artist Within discussion boards as well as contacting him directly. Mark prides himself on communicating directly with his clients and members in a timely fashion.

You can also purchase prints of his artwork at
Mark's Fine Art Prints
mark-mittlesteadt.fineartamerica.com

Mark's E-Mail Contact
markm@the-artist-within.com

Mark on LinkedIn
https://www.linkedin.com/in/theartistwithinlivingonpurpose

Facebook
https://www.facebook.com/mmittlesteadt

Mark also works with Bill Cortright and other life coaches at Bill's Stress Mastery Community. You can connect with Mark by joining him at https://www.stressmasterycommunity.com/

CPSIA information can be obtained
at www.ICGtesting.com
Printed in the USA
LVHW011540180620
658107LV00003B/182

9 781734 533507